Frank M. Elliot

History of Omega Chapter

And Reminiscences of Northwestern

Frank M. Elliot

History of Omega Chapter
And Reminiscences of Northwestern

ISBN/EAN: 9783337013776

Printed in Europe, USA, Canada, Australia, Japan

Cover: Foto ©ninafisch / pixelio.de

More available books at **www.hansebooks.com**

HISTORY OF OMEGA CHAPTER,

AND

Reminiscences of Northwestern.

A Brief Sketch of the Sigma Chi Fraternity, and a List of the Members of Omega, etc., etc.

" *The men of this fraternity who have graduated from this institution, are the men to whom we point with pride as specimens.*"—President Joseph Cummings in an address of welcome to the Sigma Chi delegates of the Fourteenth Convention on their visit to the Northwestern University.

Edited by Frank M. Elliot.

CHICAGO:
1885.

To all those who cherish college recollections, and especially to the members of Omega, whose words and deeds have symbolized the motto of our mystic brotherhood, this volume is affectionately dedicated.

PREFACE.

It is fifteen years since Omega was established. That she has a history no one will deny, and that it should be recorded in some substantial manner has also been granted. The task and the delay of compiling this history have been greatly increased by the interference of other business, and especially by the difficulty of acquiring reliable data. The record of the first five years of our existence is lost, and the information for that time has been obtained only through personal interviews and correspondence. The editor has been greatly assisted by Brother C. R. Paul, who has by his hearty sympathy with the work given valuable aid in the earlier portions of our history. He is also under obligations to Brothers Currier, E. W. Andrews, Bross, Merrick, and Wightman, and to many others in the chapter, for valuable and material suggestions. Articles contributed by members other than the editor appear over the writers' names. No attempt has been made to record all of the events that have transpired during our career, as this would require more space and labor than we have at our disposal.

In addition to the history of Omega there are included a historical sketch of the Sigma Chi Fraternity, a list of its conventions and the testimony of the worth of the fraternity by a few of the more prominent members of our order. Clustering around all these associations of the chapter, there have been many pleasant and important events to which Omega lays no particular claim, except in so far as her members have been interested in and identified with them. Some of these events are deemed of sufficient importance to be incorporated in this book. They may be considered in this connection, as they truly are, simply as college reminiscences at Northwestern.

We have attempted to make this history reliable and interesting, and with this end in view, the usual dry statistical method has been avoided as much as possible in its form and composition. This book is the record of pleasant years, a college farrago, of a few kindred minds. Members who have been individually identified with particular events and with certain periods of our history have kindly given their assistance and contributions to the work. These fragments of our history, these pleasant memories, have been gathered up and condensed into a brief space, that nothing may be lost. If this book, sent forth as a tribute to Omega and Sigma Chi, shall have the effect of renewing and increasing the affection and esteem for those "old college days" and pleasant friends, the labor which it has cost and which has been freely given will have received all the recognition that could be desired.

Fraternally yours,
FRANK M. ELLIOT.

EVANSTON, ILL., January, 1885.

CONTENTS.

Northwestern University.   *Frontispiece.*

Chapter I.
                                                                      PAGE

A historical sketch of Sigma Chi. List of Chapters.... 13

Chapter II.
The Northwestern University........................ 21

Chapter III.
Omega—A poem............................. 28

Chapter IV.
Early history of Omega............................ 30

Chapter V.
Omega reorganized; annual banquet, etc............ 38

Chapter VI.
Omega's sleigh-rides............................. 47

Chapter VII.
The Psi Upsilon movement 51

Chapter VIII.
The Boys of Sigma Chi—A song..................... 69

Chapter IX.

Some comical events at Omega—One of Knappen's stories.................................. 71

Chapter X.

Driftwood. Four college years, 1874–1878............. 78

Chapter XI.

Fratres Caros Saluto—A song..................... ...104

Chapter XII.

Omega, 1878–1879.....................................105

Chapter XIII.

History of Omega from 1879 to 1884.................108

Chapter XIV.

The Fourteenth Biennial Convention............ 122

Chapter XV.

The Northwestern District Convention of Sigma Chi....128

Chapter XVI.

Prize men of Omega. Speakers on Commencement, Class-day, Junior Exhibitions, Junior and Sophomore debates and declamations; Hinman essay and Freshmen declamation contests. Also list of the men of Omega who have occupied honorary positions, either connected with the University or the Fraternity..133

CHAPTER XVII.

The Blanchard Prize..................................143

CHAPTER XVIII.

Miscellany—The Spade and Serpent. Life-saving crew. The famous baseball team of 1871. The Velvet-Tops. King Kalakua. Wooglin and his dorg. The Greeks at Northwestern..........................149

CHAPTER XIX.

I. Fraternity Influence................................156
II. Omega Chapter House 159
III. A matter of policy 161

CHAPTER XX.

The Intercollegiate Literary Association..............164

CHAPTER XXI.

Building a gymnasium...............................171

CHAPTER XXII.

The bear story......................................182

CHAPTER XXIII.

The conventions of Sigma Chi........................201

CHAPTER XXIV.

Sigma Chi Sentiments, by Linden Kent, Psi; W. W. Fosdick, Lambda; Isaac M. Jordan, Old Alpha; John M. Hamilton, Alpha; E. L. Shuman, Omega; Ben. P. Runkle, Old Alpha; W. L. Fisher, Chi...............203

Then as now. Gleanings from old letters—J. Parks Caldwell, Alpha; T. C. Bell, Alpha; Frank H. Scobey, Alpha; John J. Piatt, George D. Prentice and Wallace Wood, Eta.................................210

Memento Mori—A poem..............................216

CHAPTER XXV.

Necrology.—Biographical sketches of the lives of deceased brothers: I. Evarts Greene Boutell; II. Fennimore Enz Hancock; III. Robert Marshall Humphrey; IV. Harry Putney Brown; V. Frederick William Randolph; VI. John S. Hancock; VII. Ezra Benedict Parrish; VIII. Frank Edward Hesler...............217

CHAPTER XXVI.

List of members, their occupation, address, etc........255

Index of names and subjects........................261

CHAPTER I.

A HISTORICAL SKETCH OF SIGMA CHI.

The Sigma Chi Fraternity was founded June 28, 1855, at Miami University, Oxford, Ohio. Its founders were six Delta Kappa Epsilons, who refused to obey the dictates of a fraternity caucus. Since there were just twelve men in the Delta Kappa Epsilon chapter, the rebellious "Dekes" could not be expelled; so the caucus members ran away with the charter and the records, while the other six stood together and became the founders of Sigma Chi. Upon an honorable adherence to what they deemed to be principles of right and justice did Sigma Chi stake her *raison d'être*. Springing from what was the most renowned and influential secret college society of the time, the founders of Sigma Chi brought to their work its tried and experienced methods and discipline. It is without doubt due to this fact of her auspicious parentage that Sigma Chi has owed much of her success. Minerva like, she sprang full-armed from the head of the fraternity Jupiter. If, however, Delta Kappa Epsilon had proven herself in some respects to be narrow and bigoted, Sigma Chi strove to broaden the principles she borrowed by embodying in them a wider justice and deeper social and friendly bonds of union. That she succeeded is attested by her thirty-eight active chapters in the best colleges of the central, western and southern states, having an average undergraduate membership of twelve, and counting a total membership roll of about 3,500 alumni members. The fraternity from its foundation had its extension in view. The older institutions of the East being already overcrowded by Greek societies, she entrusted her destiny to the rising colleges of Virginia, Pennsylvania and the West, planting her first chapter at Ohio Wesleyan University, at Delaware, in the same year with her own foundation. This was called the Gamma chapter, and on the death of the parent chapter in 1858, it assumed the government of the order. The extension of the society has resulted in the following chapters:*

No.	Date of Foundation.	Name.	Institution and Situation.
2.	1855,	Gamma,	Ohio Wesleyan University, Delaware, Ohio.
3.	1857,	Eta,	University of Mississippi, Oxford, Mississippi.

* No account is here taken of the ante-bellum chapters chartered in the South and not revived at the end of hostilities. Epsilon was chartered at the University of Nashville, in 1856; Pi at Erskine College, South Carolina, in 1860, and Sigma at Lagrange College, Tennessee, in the same year. Pi and Sigma continued till the outbreak of the Rebellion, when they were disbanded. The records of these chapters were lost or destroyed during the Rebellion.

No.	Date of Foundation	Name	Institution and Situation
4.	1858,	Iota,	Jefferson College [1871], Canonsburg, Pennsylvania.
5.	1858,	Lambda,	Indiana State University, Bloomington, Indiana.
6.	1859,	Xi,	DePauw University, Greencastle, Indiana.
7.	1859,	Omicron,	Dickinson College, Carlisle, Pennsylvania.
8.	1859,	Nu,	Washington College [1865], Washington, Pennsylvania.
9.	1859,	Psi,	University of Virginia, Virginia.
10.	1863,	Theta,	Pennsylvania College, Gettysburg, Pennsylvania.
11.	1864,	Epsilon,	Columbian University [1878], Washington, District Columbia.
12.	1864,	Kappa,	University at Lewisburg, Lewisburg, Pennsylvania.
13.	1865,	Upsilon,	Polytechnic College of the State of Pennsylvania [1876], Philadelphia, Pennsylvania.
14.	1866,	Zeta,	Washington and Lee University, Lexington, Virginia.
15.	1866,	Rho,	Butler University, Irvington, Indiana.
16.	1867,	Phi,	Lafayette College, Easton, Pennsylvania.
17.	1867,	Mu,	Denison University, Granville, Ohio.
18.	1869,	Sigma,	College of New Jersey [1882], Princeton, New Jersey.
19.	1869,	Omega,	Northwestern University, Evanston, Illinois.
20.	1871,	Chi,	Hanover College, Hanover, Indiana.
21.	1872,	Delta,	University of Georgia [1874], Athens, Georgia.
22.	1872,	Nu,	Cumberland University [1878], Lebanon, Tennessee.

No.	Date of Foundation.	Name.	Institution and Situation.
23.	1872,	Pi,	Howard College [1885], Marion, Alabama.
24.	1872,	Tau,	Roanoke College, Salem, Virginia.
25.	1872,	Sigma Sigma,	Hampden-Sidney College, Virginia.
26.	1873,	Beta,	Wooster University, Wooster, Ohio.
27.	1873,	Theta Theta,	University of Michigan, Ann Arbor, Michigan.
28.	1874,	Beta Beta,	Mississippi College [1877], Clinton, Mississippi.
29.	1874,	Gamma Gamma,	Randolph-Macon College, Ashland, Virginia.
30.	1874,	Delta Delta,	Purdue University, Lafayette, Indiana.
31.	1874,	Epsilon Epsilon,	Monmouth College [1878], Monmouth, Illinois.
32.	1875,	Phi Phi,	University of Pennsylvania, Philadelphia, Pennsylvania.
33.	1876,	Zeta Zeta,	Centre College, Danville, Kentucky.
34.	1876,	Iota Iota,	University of Alabama [1878], Tuscaloosa, Alabama.
35.	1879,	Chi Chi,	Southern University [1882], Greensboro, Alabama.
36.	1880,	Alpha Beta,	Richmond College [1881], Richmond, Virginia.
37.	1880,	Delta Chi,	Wabash College, Crawfordsville, Indiana.
38.	1881,	Kappa Kappa,	Illinois State University, Champaign, Illinois.
39.	1882,	Zeta Psi,	University of Cincinnati, Cincinnati, Ohio.
40	1882,	Alpha Gamma,	Ohio State University, Columbus, Ohio.
41.	1882,	Alpha Zeta,	Beloit College, Beloit, Wisconsin.

No.	Date of Foundation	Name	Institution and Situation
42.	1882,	Alpha Eta,	University of Iowa, Iowa City, Iowa.
43.	1882,	Alpha Theta,	Massachusetts Institute of Technology, Boston, Massachusetts.
44.	1883,	Alpha Delta,	Stevens Institute of Technology, Hoboken, New Jersey.
45.	1883,	Alpha Epsilon,	University of Nebraska, Lincoln, Nebraska.
46.	1883,	Alpha Iota,	Illinois Wesleyan University, Bloomington, Illinois.
47.	1883,	Alpha Kappa,	Hillsdale College, Hillsdale, Michigan.
48.	1884,	Alpha Lambda,	University of Wisconsin, Madison, Wisconsin.
49.	1884,	Alpha Mu,	Virginia Military Institute, Lexington, Virginia.
50.	1884,	Alpha Xi,	University of Kansas, Lawrence, Kan.
51.	1884,	Alpha Nu,	University of Texas, Austin, Texas.

In 1882, a charter was granted to certain alumni Sigma Chis in the Medical Department of the University of Louisiana to establish a chapter in that institution. After a careful investigation of the prospect in the literary department, they decided that the then occasion was not favorable for the establishment of the chapter, and the charter was returned. Such has been the territorial development of Sigma Chi—a development which, considering the high character of all the institutions entered, is without a parallel among "western" fraternities. Two of the chapters are *sub rosa*, Kappa Kappa, and Delta Delta. The latter was the means of bringing to judicial determination faculty opposition to fraternities. Its long and successful struggle with the college authorities carried up to the Indiana Supreme Court, is among the most interesting and important of Greek society annals. The living chapters are, as a whole, very prosperous. Of the defunct chapters, Delta, Beta Beta, Epsilon Epsilon, Iota Iota, and Sigma, after short but brilliant careers, disbanded by reason of faculty opposition. Nu at Washington College united with Iota when Jefferson and Washington colleges consolidated. Iota, Epsilon, Chi Chi, and Nu at Cumberland University preferred an honorable death to life with an inferior membership. Upsilon was weakened by the establishment of Phi Phi and died a natural death in the class of 1876. Sigma was first chartered in 1869 and re-chartered in 1875. The chapter at the University of Michigan was first chartered as Psi Psi in 1873 and again chartered in 1877 as Theta Theta. Phi Phi died in 1878, but was revived in 1884. There are alumni chapters at Chicago, Cincinnati; Indianapolis and Lafayette, Indiana. These hold annual and semi-annual meetings and banquets, and have the privilege of sending representatives to the biennial sessions of the Grand Chapter.

To Henry St. John Dixon, of Psi, the fraternity

system is indebted for a very unique episode. This was the organization of a chapter of Sigma Chi in the Confederate Army, known as the Constantine chapter. The chapter, whose membership, with one exception, consisted only of Sigma Chis, was established in Armstrong's brigade, of the Army of Tennessee, during the Atlanta campaign of '64. Most of the Southern colleges were closed during the war, and thus our Southern brothers sought to keep the order alive during the trying period. A touching story is told of a Sigma Chi badge manufactured from an old silver dollar with a gutta percha center and passed from one member of the chapter to another.

The publications of the fraternity consist of two editions of the catalogue, the first issued in 1870 and the latter in 1876; the "Sigma Chi Song Book," edited by a committee from Beta chapter and published in 1884; several pieces of sheet music, polkas and waltzes dedicated to the fraternity, together with various orations, addresses and poems, delivered at conventions and reunions. Perhaps, however, the pride and glory of Sigma Chi is in its magazine. For the first two years, from '80 to '82, it was conducted by the Theta chapter, since which time it has been under the editorship of Walter L. Fisher, of Chi chapter. It is truly representative, and in very many respects leads the fraternity press. A new and biographical catalogue is in preparation under the charge of Omega.

The government of the fraternity, up to the fourteenth biennial session of the Grand Chapter at Chicago in 1882, was wholly in the hands of the Gamma chapter. Her decision on petitions was almost always final, and whatever success the fraternity has enjoyed is largely due to the policy of the Gamma. Yet the development of the fraternity seemed to call for a stronger and more centralized government. This demand has been met by the last two conventions, the tendency of the reforms being in the direction of government by a judicial and legislative board of alumni members and the individual responsibility of each officer. The duties of each officer and the functions of each branch of the government are clearly defined in the constitution, which is no longer secret, and can be obtained by any member of the fraternity. The Gamma chapter now occupies an honorable position as the mother of many flourishing daughters, who have grown so strong that they have been able to erect an independent governmental structure of magnificent proportions. Gamma, after nearly thirty years of rule, finds protection again in the chapter sisterhood, and is entitled to an equal voice in all the affairs pertaining to the interest and welfare of the fraternity.   C. A. WIGHTMAN.

CHAPTER II.

THE NORTHWESTERN UNIVERSITY.

THE Omega chapter derives its strength and support from the students at the Northwestern University, at Evanston, Cook county, Illinois.

The village of Evanston is situated on the west shore of Lake Michigan, twelve miles north of Chicago. It is a village of homes, and the people who live in them are among the most advanced in social and literary circles in the West. This is so evident that the village is often called the Athens of the West. It has a population of about 7,500 people. The original settlement was called Ridgeland, and its first organized meeting was held on April 2, 1850. Like nearly every frontier town, it was composed of a drunken, immoral and villainous class of people. It was doubtless owing largely to this fact that the legal restriction in reference to the sale of intoxicating liquors within four miles of the university was incorporated in the charter. This charter was granted to the Northwestern University by the legislature of 1851. In August, 1853, three hundred and eighty acres were purchased for $25,000 by the enterprising Methodists interested in the establishment of the University.

Messrs. H. B. Hurd, F. H. Benson and A. J. Brown, the owners of adjoining property west of that purchased by the University, joined heartily with the founders of Northwestern and laid out the site for a town. On February 3, 1854, it was named Evanston, in honor of Hon. John Evans, one of the original and most enthusiastic promoters of this enterprise.

Evanston possesses many advantages aside from its educational attractions. In the first place, it is healthy. The modern improved system of sewerage, pure lake water, and fresh invigorating air are its chief advantages. Then it is a moral village. It has none of those places within its borders which tempt a young man to deviate from the line of duty and of virtue. No saloons are permitted, and as for public billiard rooms and theaters, public sentiment is against them, and they cannot exist. All the moral and social surroundings are such as to form efficient and practical safeguards so essential in a university town. Chicago, that wonderful city of enterprise and thrift, where the product of the best thought, art, business and civilization exists, is available to all those who desire pleasant and instructive recreation.

Evanston owes its creation to the religious zeal of certain leading members of the Methodist church. Its origin and the growth which has

.. been made largely by sincere labor and devotion have been guided by the kind of inspiration that presages success. What splendid foresight was exhibited in selecting this location, when we consider what educational and social advantages there are now and what possibilities there are yet open to the Northwestern University! The founders expected (and their expectations have been largely realized) to build an institution that would supply the higher and better educational wants of Chicago and of this great center.

The University was not founded, as many suppose, as a strictly sectarian institution, nor was it intended to advance one department of learning more than another. It was to be a "Christian University." The supreme design was to create a university which, if it did not teach *all* knowledge, would at least teach a number of the most desirable branches of learning. For this reason there have been added, from time to time, special departments, so that special instruction may be obtained in science, medicine, law, and music. This right of adding new departments to the University was granted to it by virtue of article seven of its charter. When the University was opened there were only two departments, the Collegiate and Preparatory. In 1869, the Chicago Medical College was made the medical department of the University. In 1873, the Evanston

College for Ladies was purchased, and co-education was introduced. The Law department was also added this year, and in 1874 the Conservatory of Music was founded. All six of these departments are under the control and direction of the trustees of the University.

The first president, Rev. Clark T. Hinman, D.D., was elected June 23, 1853; died in 1854. Rev. R. S. Foster, D.D., LL.D., was elected president June 5, 1856; he resigned in 1860. Rev. E. O. Haven, D.D., LL.D., was elected president June 23, 1869; resigned in the fall of 1872. Rev. Charles H. Fowler, D.D., LL.D., was elected president October 23, 1872; resigned in 1876. Acting presidents elected by the board of trustees. Henry Sanborn Noyes, A.M., 1860 to 1866. Oliver Marcy, LL.D., 1876 to 1881. Rev. Joseph Cummings, D.D., LL.D., was elected president July, 1881. Three of the presidents, Foster, Haven and Fowler, were subsequently elected bishops of the Methodist Episcopal Church.

The situation of the University is most admirable. It is on a slight elevation of ground in the midst of a large grove. The college campus is composed of about thirty-five acres. The trees in it are fine large specimens of oak, and are the pride and admiration of the institution. That part of the campus set aside for athletic sports is unquestionably as fine as any in this country, and with the expenditure of a small amount of money on it would be unexcelled. There are few colleges whose surroundings are equal to those of Northwestern. Bordering on the lake, with its pebbled beach and broad expanse beyond, these grounds become the favorite resort for all lovers of nature, whose delight is in the "forest primeval."

The college building is constructed of Joliet stone, and is of a rich Gothic style of architecture. Its tall and graceful spire can be seen from long distances in every direction. The building is well arranged for all the needs of the college, and is in keeping with all the great enterprises of the University. It was finished in 1869 at an expense of $120,000.

The classical, scientific and elective courses were the first to be adopted, and since then the different branches of science and philosophy have been added to the curriculum. Diplomas are issued to those persons who have successfully passed the examinations in the studies in the four-year-course required. The University was formally opened on November 5, 1855, with ten freshmen, and the first class was graduated in June, 1859, with five men. There have been about 450 persons who have graduated and gone out from the University. The total number of students in attendance during 1883-1884 in all the different departments was 753. The value of the property owned by the University is estimated at $1,500,000. A large part of this is unimproved, but the real estate being exempt from taxation, there is not the immediate and urgent necessity of selling it, especially as the property is constantly advancing in value. With the exception of the half block on which the Grand Pacific stands and a few lots on the West side in Chicago, all of the property is in Evanston. In addition to the 325 acres originally purchased, the " Billings farm " of about thirty-five acres adjoining the above tract was purchased by the University.

An erroneous idea prevails that the Garrett Biblical Institute belongs to the University. As a matter of fact the Institute was opened before the University, and was known as the Biblical Institute. In 1855 Mrs. Eliza Garrett bequeathed a large amount of property to the Institute, valued to-day at about $300,000. In honor of this munificent gift the name of Garrett Biblical Institute was substituted for the one originally given. A separate and distinct charter was obtained and the government of the Institute is under the control of an entirely different board of trustees from that of the Northwestern University. All the connection there is between the two institutions arises from a lease of about 500 feet of ground in the campus on which the buildings of the Institute stand. The Northwestern University should therefore be considered as entirely separate and distinct, as an educational institution, from the Garrett Biblical Institute. The interests of one ought not to encroach upon the right or interests of the other, and any attempt to make them conflict or to unite them in a common household on a common basis is contrary to the prudent and wise design of their founders.

CHAPTER III.

OMEGA.

SIGMA CHI has many daughters
  Scattered broad throughout the land,
But Omega is the fairest
  Of the captivating band.

Just fifteen is young Omega,—
  Young, but oh, how wondrous wise!
Brim-full is her head of knowledge,
  Brim-full to her very eyes.

She can talk in Greek and Latin,
  She can measure stars and steeps,
She can "cut you up" correctly,
  She can lay down law in "heaps."

She is wise, but not too learned;
  She with all her heart doth dote
On her quadruped companion,
  On her jolly, bunting goat.

And we love her for this mixture
  Of her wisdom and her mirth;
And we'll love her till the ending
  Of our lives upon this earth.

Aye, we'll love her long as heaven
    Grants to us her cross to bear,
And we'll love her still up yonder
    Where the crown immortals wear.

A. S. E.

CHAPTER IV.

EARLY HISTORY OF OMEGA.

OMEGA owes its origin mainly to Hon. L. C. Collins, Jr., who brought to Northwestern University the fraternity spirit he had thoroughly imbibed while preparing for college at Delaware, Ohio, and infused that spirit into the band of chosen comrades who subsequently aided him to found and maintain the chapter. It was at Delaware, too, that Bro. Collins learned to appreciate the merits of Sigma Chi, as compared with other fraternities, so that Omega actually, though in the indirect way indicated, derived its existence from the parent chapter. When Bro. Collins entered the Northwestern University as a freshman, he found but two fraternities at the institution—Phi Kappa Psi and Phi Gamma Delta—and but little genuine fraternity spirit. These two chapters had things their own way, and picked out what material they wanted at their leisure, neither finding it necessary to interfere with the other. But neither of them suited a young man who wanted to be a Sigma Chi, and Bro. Collins soon determined to organize a chapter of that fraternity at Evanston, if possible.

In those days it was a tedious process to obtain the necessary consent of the different chapters, and it was not certain that their action would be favorable. In the meantime the other fraternities were lavishing all their blandishments upon several members of the little band which Bro. Collins had gathered around him and inspired with his own ambition to be a Sigma Chi. In this emergency an opportunity was offered to establish a chapter of a new fraternity, the Kappa Phi Lambda, and advantage was taken of this as a temporary expedient for keeping the ranks of the faithful intact. The charter offered was accordingly accepted, the boys were initiated without any ceremony, and the brethren at Monmouth, Illinois, kindly loaned their badges so that the existence of the new chapter might be made known to the college world in fitting style.

Meanwhile, the correspondence with Sigma Chi acquaintances and chapters was steadily maintained, and the desired charter was finally granted, being dated June 23, 1869. This long-looked for parchment bore the names of the founders of Omega as follows:

LORIN C. COLLINS, JR., ALBERT D. LANGWORTHY,
ELLERY H. BEAL, MERRITT C. BRAGDON,
CLARENCE R. PAUL, WM. H. SPARLING,
J. FRANK ROBINSON, GEORGE LUNT.

All of these brothers, except George Lunt were present on the eventful evening when the new chapter came into being. The parent chapter had commissioned a worthy brother from Xi chapter at Greencastle, Indiana, then the nearest neighbor of Omega, to reveal to those expectant barbarians the mysteries of Sigma Chi. This brother was Edgar L. Wakeman, who had even then in his college acquired a reputation as a poet, who has since become widely known as a journalist, and is now even more favorably known as the publisher of the most ambitious literary venture of the day, *The Current*.

At that early day Evanston did not afford the advantages for holding fraternity meetings that the collegians of the present period enjoy. But the founders of Omega, animated by the spirit of the pioneer, felt free to go where they pleased, and finally settled upon the basement of the Baptist church as the most available place for coming ceremonies. Owing doubtless to the excitement naturally attending so important an event, the boys forgot to ask the trustees for the use of the church, which then stood on the corner of Hinman avenue and Church street. Possibly, however, they obtained permission of Bros. Paul and Robinson, who acted as librarians of the Baptist Sunday school, and probably carried a key to the basement. In fact, this is probably the manner in which the church came to be used for the occasion, for college tradition has it that some member of '72 usually had a key to any building or place about the University or about town that the students ever wanted to visit or use.

It was agreed by common consent that Bro. Collins should be the Grand Mogul, or whatever the official title of the High Priest of the new chapter might be, and he was accordingly initiated first by Bro. Wakeman, while the rest of the boys sat in the dark and wondered what they would have to go through. Bro. Bragdon was next called into the inner sanctum, and when he had been properly qualified, the rest followed, one at a time. Collins and Bragdon took to this new business so zealously that, with the able assistance rendered by Bro. Wakeman, they were able to make the ceremony quite interesting by the time they reached those unfortunates who were near the end of the list.

The new chapter flourished during the following year and was recognized by students and townspeople as the leading Greek organization of the institution. Additions were occasionally made to its numbers, but the greatest possible care was always exercised in their selection and the most perfect harmony invariably prevailed. The chapter was what it was intended to be, a band of brothers united by the strongest ties of affection, finding in each other the most congenial companionship, and ever anxious to advance the good name of Sigma Chi.

During the first year of its existence Omega had no settled home, and many amusing stories might be told of the devices resorted to for meetings and initiations. At that time University Hall had not been fully finished, and several meetings were held in the tower, where the boys could climb by means of ladders and feel perfectly secure against being overheard, even if they did not find roosting on the rafters in the dark very safe or comfortable. Residences in out-of-the-way places, which happened to be temporarily vacant, were often the scenes of mysterious gatherings and still more mysterious proceedings. Gowns and cowls were procured early in the history of the chapter and used with great effect on all these occasions, while the boys exhausted their ingenuity in making each initiation more interesting than any that had preceded it.

During the second year a hall was secured by renting a room in the old frame building on Davis street, in which Jno. Goebel's drug store was then located, and the chapter has since had some kind of a habitation almost without interruption. At one time the meetings were held regularly in the handsome rooms of Hesler's Gallery, then in the Haskin Block, and for some time a room in the Union Hall building was occupied. This answered well enough until initiations were in order, and then the blanket act was worked with great success either on the roof or in Union Hall. It was about this period that an aged and historical animal, known to the small boy of the village as "Jim Daly's goat," was pressed into service and occasionally assisted with becoming solemnity for a very reasonable compensation.

The chapter continued to flourish until in '70 its rivals fell into decay, and it was practically without opposition. The result of this was unfortunate. At the close of the college year, however, in June, '71, a rousing old-fashioned meeting was held, and the boys separated for their homes with the best of feeling prevailing. On reassembling after the long summer vacation a meeting was not called immediately, the intention being to take ample time for the selection of new members, as both the rival chapters had ceased to exist. When a meeting was finally held, neither the charter nor the book containing the records of all the meetings that had been held by the chapter since its organization could be found. It had been a custom to leave them in custody with the proper officer, or of any other member who happened to have better facilities for their safe keeping, and it was seldom that more than two or three members knew exactly where they were. Such valuable papers were supposed to be perfectly safe in the charge of any brother, and the others held him responsible without giving the matter any further thought. So long a time had elapsed between the time of the loss and the preceding meeting, that the boys could not agree as to who had last been seen with the charter and records, and the exact manner or method of their disappearance was never learned or satisfactorily ascertained. It was firmly believed, however, by most of the brothers, that the charter and record book had been made away with by a member who was supposed to be anxious to go into a scheme then being agitated to get another fraternity at Evanston, and who on that account wanted to break up the chapter.

Whether this supposition was true or false, the brother was expelled. The chapter was not itself afterwards, and its interests and influence languished when the large membership of '72, which had been its mainstay for several years, graduated. But, although quiescent for several months, and thought by many to be dead, Omega awoke from her long slumber on the appearance of a foe. The manner of its revival is worthy of notice, as it not only illustrates the remarkable vitality that has always characterized the chapter, but also the faculty it possessed of finding the right kind of material for membership. During the interregnum the chapter of Phi Kappa Psi had been resuscitated, and a large membership had been gathered in; and in the winter of '72 and '73 the chapter of Phi Kappa Sigma was established with a large membership. During all this time the local Alumni had been urging the reorganization of Omega, but did not succeed in having the attempt made until after both of these new chapters had taken in all the members they could find room for. It was supposed that there was no available material left, but the result simply proved the other fraternities to be very poor judges of good material. A number of the men picked up during that gloomy period of reconstruction, after the institution had been thoroughly plowed over by the two fraternities named, have been bright and shining lights in the chapter ever since, and are still as zealous in the cause as the most ardent novitiate.

C. R. PAUL.

CHAPTER V.

OMEGA REORGANIZED.

It was in the early part of February, 1873, that a meeting was called to reorganize the Omega chapter of the Sigma Chi fraternity. There were present Bros. L. C. Collins, G. E. Bragdon, F. E. Hesler, C. R. Paul, L. D. Bradley and W. E. Haskin. The only member who was then attending the University was Bro. Bradley, of the class of '74. Bros. Collins, Paul and Bragdon had received their degrees in '72, and Bros. Hesler and Haskin were engaged in mercantile pursuits in the village of Evanston.

This was the company which was to arouse the sleeping spirit of Omega and send it on its joyous mission of fraternal love and friendship. Poor Omega had lately suffered much. She not only had lost her members by graduation, and had neither hall, skull or gavel as the tangible evidence of her existence, but she had also been dealt with treacherously. Her charter, the basis of organization,—that which was in form her life and guide,—had been purloined by one of her trusted but traitorous members and given into the hands of the enemy. The records, which contained valuable minutes of the meetings ever since the organization of the chapter in 1869, were also stolen, and have never been recovered. The condition of affairs at that time was most humiliating and desperate. Nothing has ever occurred in the history of Omega which for a time so depressed her members and stopped the wheels of her progress so suddenly and effectually as this act of robbery. The rival fraternities were filled with the wildest exultation. The thing which was a secret was now known to all.

It required something of heroism for this small company to submit to this humiliation, bear the scoffs of the opposition fraternities, and not lose that spirit of fidelity, of loyalty and fraternal enthusiasm, which has so marked and characterized the work of Omega. It was a noble and courageous company, linked together with strong ties of friendship and love, which no pilfering and no indiscretion of one of its members and all of its enemies could sever or destroy. Something more than a college feud was required to divide it. The spirit of the charter remained. That could not be stolen. Animated by the highest regard for the existence and permanency of the chapter, it was now resolved by these faithful brothers to reorganize and receive, if possible, another charter from Alpha. After a vexatious delay this charter was received.

A meeting was held in Hesler's gallery, located on the second floor of the building on the southwest corner of Davis street and Sherman avenue. The officers elected were "C.," L. C. Collins; "P.," G. E. Bragdon; "A.," F. E. Hesler; "Q.," L. D. Bradley; "T.," C. R. Paul; Custos, W. E. Haskin. Just enough men to fill all of the offices. It was now determined to commence a vigorous campaign. That material could be had from the upper classes, could hardly be expected, inasmuch as the rival fraternities were supposed to have taken all the best men. But our brothers were imbued with such zeal and such realization of their need, that in a very short time members were received from all of the classes in the University, and their selection showed they had been wiser than their rivals. The third-year class in the Preparatory furnished an ample field for the selection of men, and many of us are very grateful for the privilege of thus becoming identified so early with the brethren of Omega. The term of our active membership lasted five years instead of four, as is usually the case. It was through the kindness and generosity of Bro. F. E. Hesler that we were permitted to use the gallery during this winter term and until May. It was an excellent place for these meetings. The audience-room was large and well furnished; the walls were covered with pictures and paintings, and everything partook of an air of ease and refinement quite exhilarating to the student mind. There were plenty of rooms and hallways, and sufficient fodder for the goat. The operating-room supplied the paraphernalia so necessary to the quiet and subduing effect of the initiation, and the sinuous stairway leading to the roof resounded to the uncertain step of many a victim. The chapter has never been in such luxurious rooms, and has never been so thoroughly equipped for business, as at that period. It might be added that Omega never made such progress, and was never filled with more enthusiasm than was made and received in that photographer's gallery. What was at first a weak chapter,—weak from the fact of having virtually no active men in college,—filled only with alumni and business men, became, before the year passed, a wide-awake, progressive and withal a healthy organization. Those were the days when active membership embraced all who belonged to the chapter. There were twelve men added to the chapter during the college year of '73. The date and order of entrance to full membership was as follows: February 14, Henry A. Cooper, '74; February 16, Isaac E. Lambert, '75; February 24, Daniel C. Reihl, '74; Charles P. Wheeler, '76; March 10, Charles A. Ilgenfritz, '75; March 12, Frank M. Elliot, '77; Albert D. Early, '77; March 17, Morrison M.

Gillet, '77; April 21, Alanson S. Appleton, '76; May 19, Frank A. Early, '77; June 2, Ezra B. Parish, '77; June 11, William G. Evans, '77. The last three members received only the Chi degree upon admission, but the Sigma Chi degree was conferred on each on June 16, '73.

The first of May it became necessary to procure another place for holding our meetings. It was a matter of no little importance: there were very few places available, and for the purposes of a secret society something more than an ordinary room was needed. A room was finally secured over the Postoffice. It was in an old frame building occupying the site now used for the Postoffice. It was convenient, and that was about all the merit it possessed. No initiation could be held there, the ceilings being too low for the blanket act. Such places as Hamlin's barn and the cellar of a new house on Chicago avenue, north of the big ditch, were utilized for these occasions. But for the ordinary literary and business meetings this room answered the purpose till something better could be had. New furniture throughout was necessary. The expenses were quite heavy, for these were all borne now by the members in college. The alumni were never called upon to contribute to the necessary expenditures, but they were often present and were very generous, and provided the chapter with many a substantial and pleasant extra. It was here that the custom was inaugurated of having peanuts, doughnuts and cider after the regular meetings. Sometimes oysters were served. These simple, happy occasions were more to us then than one can now imagine. They were the scenes of fervent, joyful outbursts of feeling known only to kindred spirits. The flow of wit, the hearty laugh, the eloquent words, all found a pleasant abode within these halls. It was just such fun as a student free from all care and trouble can have, and make himself and others glad. A pure recreation, stimulated by boundless hopes and magnificent possibilities. Those happy days have never been renewed by those who gathered around that festive board. How often we have longed for them and have looked forward to seasons of joy as innocent and simple as these, but they have not returned, and probably never will.

The chapter continued to grow, and the members were firmly united. The meetings were held every two weeks, and they were attended by all the members. It was only extremely urgent business, or sickness, which could prevent a brother from being present; and even then the worthy "C" would be notified of the necessity of his being absent. This was a commendable spirit, and one which long continued to be manifested in the chapter.

Again it became necessary to procure other quarters. We had outgrown our present hall, and the method required in conducting the meetings in a whisper in order that the secrets of our order might not be heard by those persons who might be outside, was alike most inconvenient and somewhat oppressive to the general interest of the meetings. Rooms were secured on the third floor in Brown's Building, on Davis street. There were two rooms, one a large assembly room and the other a smaller one, used as the "reflectory" and "armory." It was in the early part of June, '75, I believe, when we moved into them. The dedication was postponed until the 22d, when Omega had a grand reunion and banquet. It was in many respects the largest and most enthusiastic banquet the chapter ever had. There were several honorary members taken in just prior to the banquet, to enable them to participate in it; they were H. A. Pearson, F. C. Winslow and E. J. Harrison. Preparations for the banquet were very elaborate, and everything was done to make the occasion noted and to arouse public enthusiasm for Sigma Chi. This it did most successfully. The chapter hall was placed in as perfect condition as possible; fine oil paintings graced the walls; flowers and smilax deftly encircled the cross of Sigma Chi; an upright piano was secured for the occasion. This room was used for the reception. Here the ladies were introduced to the mystic signs and symbols and to the traditional goat. The large hall on the second floor was cleared for dancing, Johnny Hand, with a fine orchestra, furnishing the music. Thus were made glad the hearts and nimble the feet of the fair sons and daughters of Eve who were present. There were only twenty numbers on the programme, and every one was participated in by all who knew how to trip the light fantastic toe. Refreshments were served at a seasonable hour by a caterer from Chicago. There must have been at least sixty people present. Everything passed off delightfully and the fair name of Omega grew fairer and brighter from this joyful and pleasant occasion.

Only one thing occurred that tended to mar the completeness of this banquet. It was a trifle, a little thing; but because it was the only thing, and because it was small, it became prominent and noticeable. One of the guests, a lady, afterward engaged to a Beta Theta Pi, went to the banquet wearing the badge of the Beta Theta Pis. She wore it conspicuously and called attention to it. It was exceedingly poor taste, not to say decidedly improper, to flourish the pin of a rival fraternity at a reception given in honor of Sigma Chi. It was a firebrand of the enemy. Had our members not been perfect gentlemen, she might have spoiled for a partner to dance with, or expired for want of a dish of ice cream; as it was, she received the homage and generous treatment of true gentlemen, who sought by kindness and quiet dignity to turn the shafts of our rivals upon themselves.

It was quite late, or rather quite early, when the last note of sweet music was heard and this happy company dispersed. The gray mist of the early morn was rising from the lake, the moon and stars were growing dim, the chanticleer had just finished his morning greeting, when we "turned in" to dream of the gentle words "Good-night! Good-night! Bless you, Sigma Chi!"

CHAPTER VI.

OMEGA'S SLEIGH RIDES.

If there was one thing more than another which distinguished the years 1874 and 1875 in the history of Omega, it was the unusual number of its social gatherings. The last annual banquet had captivated the young ladies, and they were enthusiastic in their expressions of praise and admiration. The white cross was often worn by them and the general current of social thought and action was centered in Sigma Chi.

The snow was unusually deep during the winter term, and the frequent days of mild temperature offered many occasions for sleigh rides. These were readily and eagerly taken. Powers and Schwall had a large double sleigh which would accommodate thirty people, and this attached to four spirited horses was the conveyance often used. It was glorious fun. The whole chapter would turn out and secure ladies, and take a ride through the town and adjoining suburbs, singing college songs and relating college pranks, which only college-bred men and women can fully appreciate. The clear moonlight gave an increased charm to these delightful occasions. Sometimes a supper would be given and sometimes an impromptu dance would follow, and sometimes it was quite late before the fair ones were distributed among their homes or let through the back windows of the Seminary. Sleigh-riding became such a fashion that it was useless to suggest or try to have a different kind of amusement.

All went well until one night in February, when Bros. Hamline, Early and others "bethought themselves" that such a night was fit for the gods to enjoy. It was seven o'clock, and no preparations had been made. The scheme was developed in one moment and undertaken in the next. The sleigh was procured and all the boys gathered into it. "Driver!" shouted the coming judge, "make for the Fem. Sem.," and without further ceremony the party went whirling around the corner and soon darted into the yard of that attractive place. A committee was selected to wait upon the Dean to get her permission to allow the young ladies to go. It was such a dignified and diplomatic committee that it might easily have assumed the task of determining more weighty questions than the simple assent of the Dean. Its mission was successful all in particulars, the only injunction being, "Do not stay out late, but return by ten o'clock." It was then discovered that the young ladies were not in the building. They had gone to prayer meeting.

This *was* a predicament, but, nothing daunted, "Andy," the driver, was instructed to drive to the University, where the protracted meetings were being held. Fortunately the young ladies were overtaken. The question did not arise, "What would you rather do than go fishing;" but when they heard the generous invitation to "jump in," such a shout of joy went up that old Billy, with his cyclopean phiz, came around the corner of the University building to see what all this "rumpus" was about. "All right, Andy," and the party was off. "Which way, boys," he asked. "South Chicago!" shouted a trio of voices, and away they went. Everything was lovely as could be (the ladies included, of course) until near Sunny Side a sudden stop was made. Andy got out and examined the horses and harness, and discovered, so he said, that one of the traces was broken. "You will have to get out, boys, and wait till I can mend my harness," and so they did, and the young ladies, too. Nothing would be so enjoyable now as a supper. The young ladies looked at the clock. It was nearly ten o'clock. "No, they would not take supper;" "they must go right home." "The Dean would never forgive them." But Andy was not ready, and he said it would take an hour. The boys were terribly hungry, and not a little nervous. An oyster supper was given and a waltz followed.

The time passed rapidly, and a happier crowd never existed. It was eleven o'clock when the party started on its return, and it was twelve before the fair maidens were safely behind the bolted doors of the Seminary. The next day the sky was overhung with a dark hue. A storm was brewing. The Dean looked thunder and lightning. The boys quaked and the girls trembled. The day of judgment was not far off. The edict went forth, "No more sleigh rides; no Sigma Chi would be permitted to call again at the Seminary." "The Sigma Chis were no gentlemen." So said the edict, and so said some of the young ladies, who feared the scorn of authority more than they loved the friendship of Sigma Chi. This sleigh ride was the college talk for some time, and the subject was brought into the faculty meetings, but for sufficient reasons nothing more was done about it. It has always been a question whether the traces really broke or not, and whether the driver or the Sigma Chis concocted this plan for obtaining a supper and a longer ride. The reader must decide.

CHAPTER VII.

THE PSI UPSILON MOVEMENT.

THE numerous attempts to establish a chapter of the Psi Upsilon Fraternity at the Northwestern University have affected the cause of Sigma Chi as much as the combined opposition of all the established fraternities. At certain times the influence of Psi Upsilon has been most effectual in absorbing the interest and good will of our fraternity. It is pleasant for us now to look back over these struggles and contemplate what certain members of the college tried to do, and see how fortunately their plans miscarried. We do not attempt any apology for their attitude in this matter, but we are willing to present the case and leave it to the unprejudiced to determine whether the motives of these men had the correct ring to them or not. There were reasons, and justifiable ones, for the Psi Upsilon Fraternity to establish a chapter at Northwestern. It can be safely affirmed, beyond the question of a doubt, that any other chapter, whether in the Sigma Chi Fraternity or not, placed in the same circumstances, subject to the same conditions and environment, and animated by the same high motives, would have seriously considered the tempting scheme that was concocted here by the Psi Upsilon men.

There are times when the greatest good to the greatest number can be accomplished only by the dissolution of the most sacred ties. At one time such a step appeared necessary to a number of the members of the different fraternities at the Northwestern University, but their course was not sanctioned by the power which acts supremely in such matters, and the Psi Upsilon movement collapsed. No resurrection has yet occurred, and we hope none ever will. It is the history of this period, so pregnant with fraternity spirit, and especially of Psi Upsilonism, that now claims our attention. This experience in the midst of great excitement and trials will assist us, no doubt, in the future to guard better and more sacredly the honor of the cross which glistens on the breast of each Sigma Chi.

The Psi Upsilon Fraternity is justly regarded as one of the foremost in the United States. It is noted for its conservatism and for the ability displayed in certain directions, which has marked the work of the executive council and inspired the order. There are only about sixteen chapters, and these are located principally in the best colleges in the East. Its membership is large, and is principally composed of men of high culture and distinction. There are a number of its members in this vicinity. In our University there are two professors who belong to it, Robert L. Cumnock and Henry S. Carhart. It has long been the desire of the local Psi Upsilons to have a chapter established here. They appreciate more than their eastern brothers possibly can, the influence and future of our institution. In every attempt to locate a Psi Upsilon chapter here, the members to compose it have been selected from other fraternities; they being the picked men of the college. The first attempt was made in 1872.

The Phi chapter of the Phi Gamma Delta Fraternity was established in 1869, about the same time as the organization of Omega. It was composed of good men, and but for this Psi Upsilon movement it would have continued and been our strongest opponent. The matter of having Psi Upsilon represented here was laid before Phi chapter in a very tempting manner. The comparison of the two fraternities brought Psi Upsilon out in strong relief, while in their minds the Phi Gamma Delta suffered a total eclipse. This comparison, together with the florid eloquence of the declamatory professor, secured their support to the movement. As individuals, and as a chapter, they pledged themselves to Psi Upsilon. This took place at the time of the national convention of the Phi Gamma Delta fraternity at Philadelphia. Mr. James H. Raymond, '71, was a Phi delegate, and he became the grand presiding officer of the convention. More than this, it was expected that William Cullen Bryant, an honorary member of their fraternity, would deliver an address, but he was unable to do so, and at the last moment Mr. Raymond was persuaded to fill the position. This he did with a two hours' speech, and reflected much credit on his chapter and the University. When he returned with his grip-sack full of new constitutions, forms of initiation, pass-words and grips, his honors being easy, he found his chapter soul and body in this Psi Upsilon craze. With all the glory and honor acquired for himself and his chapter, his brother members preferred Psi Upsilon still.

Before ascertaining whether the executive council of Psi Upsilon would grant them a charter, they severed all connection with the Phi Gamma Delta Fraternity. They returned their charter to the home chapter with the significant note that they had found a better fraternity, and had no further use of the friendship or fraternal association of the Phi Gamma Deltas. One can imagine the reception of this bit of news after all that had recently transpired.

Their petition to Psi Upsilon was then presented, acted upon promptly, and rejected. It was a great disappointment, and one which has continued to this day. Its twenty members found little comfort in the solitude which separated them, not only from their old order, but from all the Greek fraternities. They felt the loss keenly, and especially since they were so "cordially hated" by the Phi Gamma Deltas for their ingratitude. The bond of good fellowship, which attains its highest perfection in a college secret society, was forfeited by this act, and, worse than all, has been denied to them forever.

In the spring of the year 1875 the movement for a Psi Upsilon chapter received a fresh and vigorous impulse. Under the expensive inspiration of the president, Charles H. Fowler, D.D., LL.D., the University was advertised and pushed forward at a glorious pace. A ponderous catalogue was issued, which astonished even the students when they found through it what a great institution they were attending. It proclaimed to the world that here was "a University which teaches all knowledge." This catalogue was on much the same plan as the gorgeous posters of the "greatest show on earth." There was a failure to play the bill advertised. It soon passed into history as a by-word, and is now currently known as "Fowler's $2,000 catalogue." This is only one instance of what was done under the new administration to make this University if possible to the West what Harvard and Yale are at the East. And, strange as it may appear, these cunning Psi Upsilons thought that the establishment of one of their chapters here would give the University a higher social standing, and bring more of the better class of students, such as were interested in this movement, and whose presence would be a flattering testimonial for any institution to acquire. The president was as enthusiastic in this scheme as the Psi Upsilon professors, because he thought he saw in it another means of advancing the interests of the University in the line of progress which he had so grandly formed in his mind.

A regular campaign was laid out and it was determined that nothing should be left undone to secure the coveted prize. The best cards must be played in order to win. That no enthusiasm might be lost it was necessary to act promptly and zealously. While in point of fact it was carefully planned beforehand by the Psi Upsilon men, this whole movement assumed the attitude of a spontaneous impulse. Everyone interested was to be eager to have it carried out, and that, too, in a hurry. It was a new business for a University faculty to be engaged in. It was a new and original idea for it to promulgate, that the establishment of a certain secret fraternity here would bring renown to the University, and give substantial assistance in its advancement. It was an adroit move, and Psi Upsilon deserves credit for it. It threw these boys clear off of their guard. Nothing could seem more unselfish, and nothing could appeal more strongly to college patriotism. In fact, Psi Upsilon, it was claimed, could do wondrous things for the University. The first move was to interest the Sigma Chis.

Extracts from published papers were exhibited giving accounts of brilliant receptions of Psi Upsilon, and of the prominent places occupied by her members. The high standard of the fraternity was voiced by everyone conversant with Greek fraternities. We were told how our professor in elocution was received in the different chapters where he had recently made visits. The gorgeous halls, filled with choice works of art, how they were arranged, with libraries, pianos; and a stage, where amateur theatricals were frequently given for the delectation of the members of the fraternity. Hospitality was one of the cardinal virtues of the society; and if perchance we should become Psi Upsilons in good and regular standing, and should ever visit the East, we would be received in a royal manner and feasted on the best the land could produce. The Psi Upsilon Fraternity men must be magnificent entertainers, and to mingle with them in their elegant ways and apartments must be high honor indeed.

Furthermore, we had promises of a substantial character from some of the wealthy Psi Upsilons. It was proposed to have a hall of our own, and they would see that the money would be given to pay for it. In the meantime a large room was engaged over Suhr's grocery store, which was to answer our purposes till the proposed Psi Upsilon building was completed It was evident to the student mind that to be hand and glove with the professors in the same fraternity would be of the greatest benefit. All of these questions were carefully weighed by our men; but even these would not have been considered if the relations of Omega with her sister chapters had been of a nature to draw forth a greater amount of fraternal spirit. There was no Sigma Chi magazine published at that time, and the fraternity had not fully recovered from the effects of the war and reconstruction. There was scarcely any visiting done between the different chapters, and the government of the fraternity by one chapter was far from satisfactory. We were the only chapter of the fraternity in the state, and were, to many intents and purposes, isolated, so that our allegiance to our own fraternity was easily shaken by these glowing prospects held up before us. 'It is true a correspondence was kept up with a few of the chapters, but it was meager and quite unsatisfactory. There seemed to be nothing outside of our chapter to arouse a cordial discussion of the methods of conducting a fraternity, or to enlist a hearty interchange of ideas. We were, in fact, surrounded only by the ties of our own brotherhood. The sum and substance of the whole affair was, the Sigma Chi Fraternity did not appear to offer the full measure of present good and future greatness which the glorified vision of Psi Upsilon did, and we consented to become Psi Upsilons, if we were properly solicited, and if we could sever our connection with Sigma Chi in a fair and honorable manner, but the solicitation was to come first.

Very suddenly, and in a mysterious manner, Professor Carhart went to New York to present the matter before the executive council, and have a committee appointed to come here and investigate and report on the feasibility of the establishment of a chapter. The mission was more than successful, and forthwith a committee of two was appointed, one member of it a graduate of Yale, and the other of Amherst. The professor returned filled with high hopes of the success of the scheme. It was determined to start off with a good large chapter. One of the conditions required by our brothers who were interested in this movement, if it proved successful, was that *all* of the members of Omega should be adopted into the Psi Upsilon Fraternity. The active men would not consent to be separated from those who were nearer to them than brothers or sisters. There was no objection to this, as all of our men were considered good enough material for Psi Upsilon. But the members of the other fraternities were regarded with less favor. They had some choice men, but they also had a great many quite undesirable, if not objectionable, persons. Those who were selected and who were in happy accord with the whole project were J. A. J. Whipple, Lucius L. Coleman, and William L. Martin, of the Phi Kappa Sigma, and John Jacob Crist and Thomas C. Warrington, of the Beta Theta Pi. There were altogether about twenty five students and graduates interested in this movement. They were all, as Judge Tourgee said of the Revolutionary Fathers, "bang-up good men," and would have made an exceptionally strong chapter.

The committee from New York, upon its arrival in Chicago, was taken to the Grand Pacific hotel and was quartered in the princely rooms generally used by the presidents, lords, and distinguished persons, when stopping there. It was quietly and modestly stated that the Northwestern University owned the land on which this palatial hotel was built, and that the rental in

1890 would be something fabulous. The committee spent a number of days in looking over the city, examining the merits and possibilities of the University, and testing the social qualities of the prospective members of their fraternity. The president of the University treated the project with unusual good grace, and extended to the committee a cordial hospitality. He entertained the committee with a private and elaborate dinner, at which a number of the most active persons interested in the scheme were present. The night previous to the committee's departure a grand banquet was given at the old Lakeside hall. There were present all the Psi Upsilon men who could be found within a radius of twenty miles of the village. Our crafty president was there to manipulate the train of thought and to entertain the company with his famous stories. Distinguished Psi Upsilons paid glowing tributes to their fraternity, and with becoming grace spoke pleasantly of the men whom they hoped to call brothers. It was a brilliant affair, and the feeling displayed on the subject of Psi Upsilon was noticed to be particularly harmonious. Toasts were given, college glees were sung, and the whole evening was consumed in a most convivial manner. The reception of the committee and all the attending negotiations were thus far satisfactory. The committee expressed the highest admiration for the men whom it had met, and for the geneious and delightful entertainment provided for it. It was filled with the highest praises in our favor. In its estimation the University was good enough for Psi Upsilon. It really thought our men would be an honor, a great acquisition, to its fraternity. This was all very nice. It was pleasant to be considered worthy of such high honor.

Let no one, however, imagine that the committee escaped a searching examination concerning the merits and demerits of the fraternity it represented. It was essential for our men, especially, to obtain and verify all the information possible of that fraternity before they would take the final step of withdrawing from the Sigma Chi Fraternity. The committee was asked what report would be made in the matter. Its reply was very favorable, everything that could be asked. In fact, it desired the report to be as strong a document in our favor as possible. It was suggested that Professors Carhart and Cumnock should write the report. The case could not be made too strong, and the committee would adopt it. With this masterly document, the combined effort and free gift of our learned professors, the committee departed. The impression it left was, that there was no question of the final success of the movement.

Preparations were to be made for going to Ann Arbor, where there was a large and efficient chapter of Psi Upsilon, to have the mystic initiation performed. Hon. Perry H. Smith, of Chicago, tendered the use of his private car for conveying the party when the time should arrive. The last of June, after commencement, was the time set for the grand pilgrimage. The committee reported to the executive council, and then it became necessary to have the affirmative vote of every chapter. The report of the vote of each chapter as it came in was sent here at once. Everything looked hopeful. The affirmative vote was received from twelve chapters, then came three negative votes, the only opposition made, in the fraternity. A special report was prepared and sent to each of the three chapters voting no, asking for a reconsideration of their votes. This was done by two chapters, which then voted affirmatively. One chapter still voted no. It was, let it be known, Iota Chapter, at Kenyon College, Gambier, Ohio. All the pressure and influence, outside of a moneyed consideration, was brought to bear on this chapter, but it was of no avail. Its action had every appearance of being a clear and decided case of obstinacy and spite. The chapter was unquestionably the most insignificant in the fraternity. It was nearly dead, and, in fact, did die within a year from that time.

It would be difficult to express the indignation felt over this provoking defeat. Dr. Fowler wanted the most wicked man in town employed to swear for him. The air assumed a sulphurous hue whenever the affair was mentioned. The Psi Upsilon men here had been treated shabbily, and they did not hesitate to show the depth of their indignation and chagrin. It was some time before the affair could be talked of in a simple, philosophical manner, and looked at in its proper light. The deed was done and there was no remedy. The feelings of Omega's members were mildly lacerated. They were not filled, however, with the same depth of disappointment and profane anger that stirred the other interested parties. The enthusiasm for Psi Upsilon soon vanished. A reaction took place, and there were many things said that plainly showed that her faults had been fully noticed. Interest in Sigma Chi increased, and it seemed better adapted to the wants and purposes of our chapter than ever before.

Through this intense excitement and disappointment there came wisdom to Omega. She realized what was never fully appreciated before, the moral hazard in attempting this change. The oaths taken in Sigma Chi are obligatory for all time; and as we now regard the matter, nothing can be more difficult than to effect a change from

Sigma Chi to another fraternity. If our vows are of any force whatever, this cannot be done, unless, perchance, one is expelled. A Sigma Chi cannot join another fraternity without committing moral perjury. The whole question rests on the quality of this moral obligation. Our fidelity to the fraternity is required through adversity as well as through prosperity, through trials and disappointments, youth and old age. This question of fidelity, which was guaranteed by solemn oaths, would have been presented when the time came for separation, and on this rock the chapter would have gone in pieces. In the enthusiasm and zeal for the new movement, the question did not arise, but the chapter would have had to meet it and determine the value of these oaths. It is fortunate the matter did not take this issue. It was fortunate, too, for Omega and Sigma Chi that the Psi Upsilon movement failed just when it did. No one here was to blame. There were no dissensions within or without the chapter. Finally the conditions of invitation presented to the men here to enter the Psi Upsilon fraternity were never completed, and they withdrew from the compact, without loss of honor, and without causing their fraternities to suffer at the hands of their Greek opponents.

As we contemplate the two fraternities to-day, we are not sorry one whit that the movement failed. The Psi Upsilon fraternity is, as has been said, conservative—conservative to the extent of being aristocratic. Like all aristocracies, wealth is the sum and substance of its existence. This movement is an example of how one chapter may defeat the combined wish of all the other chapters, no matter how wise or how prudent the cause may be. It is a serious defect in her form of government, but she is so conservative that she would never think of modifying or liberalizing it. Then Psi Upsilon is an Eastern fraternity. No great crime, we admit, but to Western young men, whose lives have been cradled in this great West, and who expect to remain here and grow up with the people and the great enterprises centered here, a Western fraternity is far preferable for them to join. They will find many more men of the Western fraternities than they will of those belonging to an Eastern fraternity like Psi Upsilon. The benefits and emoluments derived from fraternities are not restricted to college halls; we find their influence in all the walks of life, and they have become a power for good and a means of success to many a graduate in his after-college career. In all this Western empire these young men will find through the influence of the Western fraternity easy access to social and professional advancement. One of the honored disciples of Psi Upsilon boasts of the fact "that nothing is known of his fraternity." We quote from the official magazine of the Psi Upsilon fraternity, which exhibits its peculiar conservative policy in another form: "We announce as an established policy of the *Diamond*, not to exchange with any fraternity journal. * * * Psi Upsilon has formed her policy independent of any fraternity for fifty years, and will continue the same course fifty years longer, as far as the *Diamond* is concerned. Exchanging is one of the first stages of panhellenism, with which we have no sympathy whatever." It is seldom one finds a fraternity which courts oblivion in this way. In comparison with the progressive Greeks, it must be candidly admitted that Psi Upsilon has relatively lost ground.

On the other hand, Sigma Chi has won steadily by her strict regard for principle, and by cultivating the higher and nobler qualities of the heart and mind. She is now under the most unique form of government known in the history of fraternities. She has shown remarkable energy and discretion in the management of her affairs, and in this way she has acquired an honorable position among the leading Greek fraternities of the United States. Being so strongly represented in the West and South, she commends herself most favorably to the young men of these sections of the country. *The Sigma*

Chi, the official magazine of the fraternity, is not only recognized by our members as being of incalculable value to them, but is regarded with the highest favor by its cotemporaries. It stands in the first rank of the Greek society publications, and is a worthy index of the progressive and high-standard policy of the Sigma Chi Fraternity.

Sigma Chi has enlarged her field of operation by establishing chapters in colleges where there are men qualified to honor and strengthen the fraternity. Her history for the past decade has been one of wonderful achievements, and we may safely hope, without doubt of its fulfillment, for greater and better results to come during the next ten years.

CHAPTER VIII.

THE BOYS OF SIGMA CHI.

Tune—"Last Cigar."

Come, gather now, my brothers all,
  And raise your voices high,
Till all around repeats the sound,
  Hurrah for Sigma Chi!
What though life's storms may buffet us?
  Their fury we defy;
For here's a band will by us stand,
  The boys of Sigma Chi.

Chorus:
  The boys of Sigma Chi, the boys of Sigma Chi,
    For here's a band will by us stand,
  The boys of Sigma Chi.

Though all that glitters is not gold,
  And fickle friends may fly,
We find no dross where shines the cross
  Of glorious Sigma Chi.
When doubt and danger gather round,
  With trust we will rely
Upon the breast whereon doth rest
  The cross of Sigma Chi.

Chorus:
  The cross of Sigma Chi! we ever will rely
    Upon the breast whereon doth rest
  The cross of Sigma Chi.

And now we pledge our lady friends,
   Whose smiles are our delight;
Their voices clear enchant the ear,
   Their faces charm the sight.
With joy we haste those friends to meet,
   The parting costs a sigh;
May fortune rare attend the fair,
   The friends of Sigma Chi.

Chorus:
   The friends of Sigma Chi, fair friends of Sigma Chi;
     May fortune rare attend the fair,
   The friends of Sigma Chi.

Our future life may sever us,
   Our paths be far apart,
Yet mem'ries dear will draw us near,
   In union of the heart.
And though our future cares and ills
   We'll meet with courage high,
Our hearts will pine for Auld Lang Syne,
   And glorious Sigma Chi.

Chorus:
   For glorious Sigma Chi, for glorious Sigma Chi;
     Our hearts will pine for Auld Lang Syne,
   And glorious Sigma Chi.

W. M. BOOTH, '78.

CHAPTER IX.

SOME COMICAL EVENTS AT OMEGA.

There have occurred some humorous and laughable events in the history of Omega. Brief mention may be made of a few. One evening, when Bro. Gillet was being made familiar with the antics of the goat, it was determined that no boisterousness should be allowed. Everything must be done in a quiet manner, and if possible at a certain time a studied and death-pervading silence must be produced. At this particular time Bro. Cooper, who was a splendid musician, and who could play a tune on almost everything, from a piano to a piece of stovepipe, undertook to play on a glass funnel which was used in the gallery for filtering nitric silver. He succeeded in finishing his pet tune amid the bursts of laughter of his brothers. The acid, however, had not been entirely removed from the funnel, and some of it got on his lips and face. The joke developed the next morning in the blazing sun, when he found a beautiful black ring around his mouth and black spots here and there on his face. These he carried several days, to the amusement of all his friends who knew the cause thereof.

Whenever anything new in the way of amusements was found, it was always brought to the society hall to be tested. The roller skates were coming into fashion, and it happened that A. D. Early was there that night. He tried them, and tried hard, but somehow or other he could not manage them. He cut all the fancy figures, and runs too. Those who saw him will never forget it. It seems as if there was more side-splitting laughter then than ever before or since in the society.

Policeman Carney was a terror to the students in former years. One night, when several of the Sigma Chi boys were taking a walk near the Lighthouse, one of them shouted to C. T. Drake, who was lagging behind, that Carney was coming. Well, if you could have seen him! He literally plowed the ground for three blocks. He must have tumbled down half-a-dozen times in his attempted flight from the grim clutches of the constabulary. First he went down in a ditch, then over a fence, then he bit the silent earth, and finally, from sheer exhaustion, he landed prostrate in a patch of mullein stalks. It will always excite a laugh from all those who remember the scene. The funny part of it all was, that Carney was not within a mile of the place.

C. W. Draper was very fond of horses, and always seemed to enjoy the nice appointments of a good stable. Bro. Hamline had a barn, in which he had a stud of horses to be proud of. The "hatchway" was particularly useful, and the manner of feeding the horses was so unique that Mr. Draper was given a private exhibition of the many features of this excellent stable. He said afterwards that the "fodder act" was the best he had ever seen.

Omega has had some wonderful men, but without exhibiting any preferences we may be excused for mentioning the astounding feat that Frank E. Knappen once performed. I think it was the first time he was in the hall. In order to bring out the qualities and excellencies of strangers, the boys used to have them do some little thing, as climb a door, or walk down a ladder head foremost, or dance a jig in a stretched blanket. These are all very pleasant parlor amusements, and it is surprising they have not been found outside of college precincts. But Mr. Knappen had artistic aspirations. He wanted to fresco the ceiling of the hall with his feet; and when one remembers his unusual length, the act does not seem at all preposterous. But even his lengthy legs were unable to do him the service he so earnestly desired, and it was necessary to call in the aid of his friends. The contrivance used was a blanket. They laid Mr. Knappen out in this and, with brush in one hand and his pallet of colors in the other, he prepared himself for the novel expedition to the ceiling. The boys gathered around and tossed him up a number of times, and every time he shot up, with the most accelerated movements he was able to paint a perfect picture. He gave a scriptural name to every picture he made, and it was remarkable what a fund of names and subjects he produced. These frescoes, by the process of age, have become imbedded in the ceiling, and are only partially visible to-day.

In matters of ceremony, Bro. A. D. Early has probably never had an equal in our chapter. He had a commanding presence, and his utterances were marked with an emphasis and an originality that have left their impressions to this day. He was a custos at one time, an officer of dignity and honor. He was doing his interrogatories in a very satisfactory manner, when some one sprang a college joke, or "chestnut," on him. He had started, "Is he a worthy," etc., but at that point he could not restrain from laughing, and he had the merriest and heartiest laugh, too. Out it came, a bursting, bubbling shout. "Is he a worthy boo, who, who?" Then everyone else boo, who, whoed, and made the welkin ring. This boo, who, who business was immediately adopted, and has supplied its portion to the fund of mirth ever since.

ONE OF KNAPPEN'S STORIES.

Greek Lexicons "came high" in 1873 and 1874, when the class of '77, at the Northwestern University were needing the services of the same in college, and I have no doubt they do now, for that matter. I had a chum in those days named J. D. Andrews, of the same class, who was called "Deck" for short. We needed a complete, full and unabridged lexicon for use as above indicated, and we both tried to purchase second-hand ones if they were in fairly good condition, and save the large amount necessary to become the sole proprietors of a bran-new one from the bookstore. The price of them new was $5.40. I hunted some time, made numerous and vain inquiries, and finally bought a new one for the price stated.

One day "Deck," who did not know exactly the price of them when new, but only knew they were expensive, came home with a smile all over his face, and so pleased about something that he did not know how to begin to express himself. I said: "Deck, what's the matter?" He said: "I have made a bargain that *is* a bargain," and throwing a large bundle upon the bed, said: "Look at that." I took the bundle up, took off the wrapper, and saw it was a second-hand Greek lexicon. It was not as good as new, because the cover on one side was off, the leaves torn out without any apparent plan or system, and those that were left were covered with fly specks so generally that many words were entirely illegible, and others seemed to be made up of a succession of i's. I looked it over, and said: "Deck, where did you find it?" "Find it!" said he, "Hades, I bought it, and got it cheap, too. That saves paying full price when one takes time to look around a little." The lexicon had tags on the margin, at the beginning of each letter, to assist one in finding and turning to the words readily. New ones did not have these tags. Some of the tags had, however, outlived their usefulness and "gone hence." I looked at it again, and while examining it, it slipped out of my hands and about forty-eight leaves came out, the back of the book being weak and somewhat exhausted. I gathered the ruins up and laid them on the bed, and said I: "Deck, how much did you give for the—the—the—bundle?" "Why," said Deck, "I only gave $6.25 for it!" "Why," said I, "new ones cost only $5.40!" Deck looked me in the face and, driven by the extremities of the situation to some justification for an apparent foolish purchase, blurted out: "Well, great Scott, don't you see them tags?" His profanity was undoubtedly induced, and perhaps partially excused, by Deck's feelings of chagrin and disappointment. He heard the story told before his course in college was finished, if I remember right, 1,639 times. It is but fair to say that others enjoyed it even more than Deck did, as it was invariably told in his presence. Deck is now a physician, if I am correctly informed, and as he stood first-class as a student, I am sure he ranks high in his profession. While I have told this story before, yet I am sadly conscious that I have omitted many interesting and material details connected therewith, and if no one else will, I am absolutely certain that "Deck" will forgive me for leaving them out. Deck also denied that he was guilty of the use of the euphonious but ungrammatical expression, "them tags," but it was told so often that it seems now as if I could hear Deck speak the very words themselves, but it may be from frequent repetition of the story.

CHAPTER X.

DRIFTWOOD — FOUR COLLEGE YEARS, 1874–1878.

My thoughts run back in a day-dream of almost forgotten events. The driftwood goes floating by, scattered and shifting and fragmentary, leaving its stranded recollections. The picture must be incomplete and full of errors, but it is fixed in my mind; I cannot alter it now.

I—SIGMA CHI, 1874–75.

The college year of 1874–75 opened auspiciously for Omega. The Northwestern University was reaping, in a large attendance, the fruits of Fowler's energetic management. A far-sighted person might even then have suspected that a collapse was imminent, but no sign of the coming reaction as yet appeared upon the surface of events. There was a feeling of buoyancy in all minds, and a sense of rising importance with a vague expectation of greater progress yet in prospect. It was the genius of the commanding general which inspired all this. A few years later, when Fowler's policy had proven a Moscow campaign of defeat and disaster, the ambitious leader had already gone to new fields, and other hands had to bear the labor and discouragements of a retreat to safer ground.

But in the fall of 1874 there were twelve hundred students in the various departments. The newly founded college of technology was in motion with good professors of chemistry and civil engineering, and *bona fide* engineering, and technological students in abundance. The scientific and modern language courses were also veritable separate departments, and were well officered and well attended. Of Professors Allyn, Metcalf and Cooley, the genial trio of talented young men who managed the engineering course, the memory has almost passed away in the college halls. Prof. Cooley is now editor and part owner of the Chicago *American Engineer*. Prof. D. H. Wheeler taught English literature. His son, Chas. P. Wheeler, was a junior and a member of Omega when the writer of this was a freshman novitiate into Sigma Chi. This is remembered chiefly because it was through him that badges were secured on payment of suitable ducats, and thus the consuming ambition of the new member was satisfied, and he became an object of admiration to himself and a Sig in full uniform. Charles P. Wheeler, '76, was not so formidable a Tribune as his cynical bearing had led some younger members to suppose. He was as genial as any, when well acquainted. At that time he was with

Krantz, '76, editor and proprietor of the *Tripod*, and had among his classmates a high reputation as a writer, but not as a speaker. It was believed that he wielded the pen with more than common talent, and that literary or editorial work would be his ultimate career. He is now a successful business man in Chicago. In New York he assisted his father in conducting the *Methodist*, a religious paper, but never engaged in journalism as a profession.

Pari passu, with the prosperity of Northwestern University rose and fell the fortunes of our chapter of Sigma Chi. At this time both were at the highest point of prosperity ever reached. Omega then had eighteen members pretty evenly distributed in the classes. Early in the term Harris, Booth and E. W. Andrews were initiated from the freshman class, and no other members of '78 were subsequently admitted. In the junior year, Demorest, formerly with '77, joined this class, and with them took his degree.

Sigma Chi held the supremacy in social matters, as it always has done, from the fact that so many of her active and alumni members reside in Evanston. The year of which we are writing owed most of its festivities to the management of our various members. Innumerable receptions, weddings, sleigh rides, and amateur dramatic entertainments, public lectures and concerts flourished under Sigma Chi patronage. All this could not have transpired through the exertions of the eighteen active members, who were at the same time winning a lion's share of college honors. It was the result of the joint action of the alumni and all our lady allies of Evanston. The memorable sleigh ride mentioned on another page was among the writer's first experiences of the spirit of daring which pervaded all our actions. It cost us rather dear in one respect. Our names were put upon the black list at the Woman's College, and we were not permitted to call. The wedding of Bro. B. F. Martin, of Alpha, to Miss Creighton, of Evanston, was hailed by the chapter as a fitting occasion to indicate both our esteem for the young lady and her family, and to entertain our visiting brother. Our formal appearance as a chapter, with the family at the Methodist church, where the public ceremony was performed, and at the marriage reception later, was long remembered by us with pleasure. Out of this happy event grew another in the form of a reception to the chapter and our lady friends, tendered by Mrs. Butler, with whom we had been associated in the wedding arrangements of Bro. Martin. A reception to our friends in town was that year given in Sigma Chi hall, which was especially decorated for the event. Certain unsightly paraphernalia was carefully stowed and locked up out of sight in one of our small rooms, and the rest of our quarters thrown open. One of the waggish sophomores had procured a goat from a well-known source. The animal was actually kept on an upper landing, in plain sight, all the evening, and was naturally the cause of much curiosity and merriment. Our hall was well furnished, but upon this evening its walls were also beautified with pictures, loaned from private residences. It has never since quite equaled that night in splendor; in fact, it has never since been thrown open, although several larger and more elaborate receptions have been given by the chapter.

New members from nearly all the classes were that year added to our roll, including Taylor, '76, and Henry Frank, a Jew by birth, but later a member of the Methodist church and an eloquent minister. Both were phenomenally brilliant students, and took all the prizes within reach. Taylor subsequently conferred honor upon the University, as well as the Sigma Chi Fraternity, by taking two prizes at the inter-collegiate contest at New York. It was thought remarkable that Western colleges should hold their own in competition with the older institutions of the East; and, as we alone among fresh-water colleges attempted this, general attention was drawn to the Northwestern University. It is proper here to mention that we received four prizes at the Eastern contests, Miss Lizzie Hunt and Frank Hills taking one each for essays. Henry Frank spent his sophomore year at Harvard, taking a valuable prize while there, but subsequently rejoined his class. He was married to a classmate, Miss Cleveland, before leaving Evanston for his field of duty.

We freshmen saw with regret the last of '75, including Hamline, who had taken the Hurd prize, and was a contestant for the Blanchard prize. Frank M. Harris, and James B. Norris, Draper, Webster, Ilgenfritz and Lambert, also of '75, did not finish their college course at the Northwestern University.

Another familiar face which we did not again see was that of Daniel C. Riehl, '74, who as an alumnus had still taken a most active interest in, our affairs and attended all our meetings.

When we returned in the fall, another member was also absent, this time from the active membership. Robert M. Humphrey, '77, died before the fall term opened.

Knappen, '77, was also made a member during this year. He was afterwards one of our most active workers and a marked character. Like Evans, of the same class, he was fond of athletics, and especially baseball, and always was expected to be a member of the nine sent out to struggle for the "silver ball" of the inter-collegiate contests. Knappen was a rare mimic and vocalist. He was the only successful "warbler" then in college. We believe there are never more than one or two in any college, and they are always in demand. We considered Bro. K. the equal of the "warblers" of the Yale or Amherst glee clubs, which sang in Chicago.

The Grand Chapter or biennial convention of '74 was attended by Bro. Dan. Riehl, who acted as Omega's delegate. His verbal reports were full and interesting, but somewhat in contrast with those we now obtain through our enterprising journal, *The Sigma Chi*, and our efficient general secretaries.

II—SIGMA CHI '75-6.

The opening of the next year saw many new members added to our roll. From the class of '79 N. S. Davis, Jr., D. P. Donelson and E. McWilliams were at once initiated. During this year also our new hall, which had been arranged with deadened walls, etc., for our use was occupied. The change was in reality not beneficial, since our new headquarters were not so central in location, and therefore not so convenient as a place of resort. The new rooms were in Shaw's block, near the station, while the old ones were in Union Hall block. This latter large hall occupied so much of the building that we were almost the only tenants, and used to monopolize everything above the ground floor, even taking possession of the auditorium when we chose. The same may be said of the roof of the building, which had a parapet waist high on the side toward the street. As the structure was three stories above the sidewalk, we felt safe from eavesdroppers. It was an ideal building for initiations, with its great empty hall, its long stairs to an alley, and its ladder and scuttle to the roof. We had complete control of the latter, as they were on our private landing. What scenes were enacted in that building by some, who are now grave teachers, legislators and professional men, no living being outside of our order ever knew — except Jim Daly's goat. This useful and once celebrated member is now dead, it is reported. May he rest in peace! On one occasion, when James McWilliams, '80, had ridden him home after a hard night's work, he neglected to settle promptly for his hire, and early the next day the owner started to collect his customary fee. Accosting certain members of the Phi Kappa Sigma, he demanded his pay for the goat which "You fellers had up there last night!" and named the gentleman with whom he had negotiated. To say that these rivals were jubilant at having made this discovery is putting it very mildly. Thinking that they had scored a point, they published it widely. Our members took it coolly, however, and, in reality, rather enjoyed the notoriety thus obtained, although vexed at first. We were in most matters on terms of good fellowship with the Phi Kappa Sigma. Their membership was good, but small, on account of the youth of the chapter. During this year they increased the membership to twenty or more, making it rather heterogeneous. Their large, fine hall adjoined the single small room used by the Beta Theta Pi. The Phi Kappa Sigma hall was lighted only from the top, and was surrounded by closets, so as to give it double walls. From one side the plastering was cut away in the closet and very minute holes were made into the plastering of the Beta Theta Pi's room, so that all the proceedings could be seen and heard. All regular meetings were thus regularly witnessed, and when initiations were in order, some other fraternity men were occasionally invited to see the fun. A few Sigs saw the initiation of John Bannister and one other. The members of both Sigma Chi and Phi Kappa Sigma agreed that the "ceremony" was the most inane and disgusting show ever witnessed; utterly devoid of humor or play of true wit such as enlivens most college pranks, that otherwise would appear coarse. The performance, which lasted but a short time, was more characteristic of the heavy fun of a country barroom than of the atmosphere of culture which men of education create. It was not even on a par with a third-rate Masonic or Odd Fellows' initiation. No wonder that Eastern college men occasionally get a poor opinion of Western standards of mind and training!

A movement to erect and equip a gymnasium was one of the results of Sigma Chi energy during this year. This was not a fraternity affair, but a general one. Its three promoters, Taylor, Lunt and Evans, were Sigs, however. The latter two gentlemen gave several hundred dollars apiece to ensure success. Through the enormous personal effort of Taylor $3,000 were finally raised among the students, and the present building put up and furnished. It was at first a stock company and governed by directors. Subsequently the charge of it was given to the trustees of the University. The bowling alley was the gift of the Omega chapter, as is now testified by the marble slab. The alley cost $250.

In the Preparatory we saw unusual opportunities for securing good material from the third-year class, and departed from our usual custom so far as to admit Bros. W. L. Brown, J. W. Bennett, James E. Deering, John E. Lipps and Frank Dale before the end of the year. This was a move we never regretted, as it gave us an unquestioned hold upon '80, which we never lost. From this class we soon after secured Jessup, Foulkes, C. D. Etnyre, J. W. McWilliams and H. A. Smith, making ten members in all. The year closed prosperously with college prizes in all classes. Our outgoing seniors, Taylor, Matthew and Appleton, took three out of five of the Hurd prizes, for best essays, and the two former divided the oratorical one-hundred-dollar prize. These honors, with those already mentioned, gave Taylor an enormous reputation as a "bright" man. He is now a professor at Albion College, Michigan. Hilton and Matthew, of the same class, are filling Methodist pulpits. Al. Appleton is a Chicago journalist, and C. P. Wheeler is a coal dealer in the same city. Besides the gymnasium enterprise, which has been mentioned as essentially a project of Omega's members, two rather amusing escapades occurred during this year, one of which has always been unjustly laid at the doors of Sigma Chi. It was in fact an impromptu affair, in which a few of the college men were engaged with a number of the town boys. The first of these, which occurred January 17, 1876, was a somewhat irregular and unexpected reception tendered to the Hon. Schuyler Colfax, who had delivered a lecture in the village. The reception he received must have forcibly reminded the dignified vice-president that he was in the wild, harum-scarum West, unless perhaps, recollections of his own college days tempered his judgment. The Beta magazine for February, 1876, discoursed as follows:

"The Hon. Schuyler Colfax, who is a wholesouled Beta, lectured in Evanston, Ill., and after the lecture he was invited by the members of the Alpha Rho chapter to attend a chapter meeting and partake of the 'canine' with them. Schuyler never refuses an invitation of this kind, and he accordingly met with the boys. Immediately upon his arrival at the chapter room, a mob, consisting of members of the Sigma Chi and Phi Kappa Sigma fraternities, assembled in the outer halls, howling, singing and conducting themselves more like fiends than like students 'having a high sense of honor.' This was kept up throughout the meeting, and when, at its close, Mr. Colfax, attended by the members of Alpha Rho, started for his lodging place, the front doors of the building were found to be tied. The party, however, made their *exit by the back door* [italics our own]. Arrived at the outside, Bro. Colfax delivered an extemporaneous lecture to the mob, which, for point and pungency, excelled even his brilliant platform efforts. The rioters disclaimed any intent to insult Bro. Colfax, but said they meant to 'go for the Beta chapter.'"

This is a moderately truthful account of what occurred, from a Beta standpoint. The crowd had assembled mainly from curiosity to see the noted visitor. A number of persons in it were lodgers in the building (Hoag's) in which was the small Beta room upon the top floor. The locality was so central that a crowd could not but collect at a moment's notice. Although a few afterward made apologies to Mr. Colfax for having participated in this affair, it is obviously impossible that more than a small fraction of a crowd of a *hundred* or more could have been of the opposition fraternities, whose combined membership was not over *thirty-five*. The nervousness and silly behavior of two or three officious Betas were the only causes of what little disturbance took place. One hare-brained young man in particular, whose conceit and general immaturity had made him the subject of a mock-programme joke, was seen repeatedly to rush to the landing above and threaten vengeance upon the crowd below, probably to the disgust of his more sensible companions. Seeing that one or two were "losing their heads" without good reason, the disposition to "guy" them could not be restrained.

Good-natured chaffing went on for a time, and a large crowd gathered in the hallways, stairs and on the sidewalks. In reply to any particularly abusive language from above, complimentary offerings of one sort or another were from time to time seen to fly upward toward the top landing. No one ventured near their door or even upon the same floor, although they had a perfect right to do so in a public building. In fact, no one would have dreamt of molesting the meeting, had not one or two self-important fellows precipitated a row by rushing out to insult those who had not yet done anything to give real offense. A leading Beta acknowledged this afterward.

When it was desired to withdraw to their homes the members found the crowd so great, and reported so hostile, that they sneaked out the *back door*, as their own account states.

Herein they made an almost incredible mistake for supposed men of honor. Had they taken it for granted that their manhood would be respected, and walked boldly into the crowd and through it as they had a right, not a hand would have been raised to molest them, nor a word of disrespect been heard by their guest. It is safe to say that no fifteen or twenty Sigma Chis, gathered together, would be stopped by any crowd or mob from going where they felt they had a right to go, unless the said mob was prepared for a bloody fight, instanter, on the spot.

It was an indignity to Mr. Colfax to sneak out with him like a criminal among the cobwebs and ashpits of the back area. He must have left Evanston with an utter contempt for the pusillanimity of the Betas, for he has never since visited them.

Arrived at last upon the sidewalk from this roundabout trip, Mr. Colfax did as quoted, "deliver an extemporaneous lecture."

"Young man!"

"Sir?" replied a gigantic sophomore, Simon Peter Douthart, who towered head and shoulders above the great politician.

"When you grow up you will live to regret this, sir!"

Next morning Mr. Colfax shook the dust of Evanston forever from his sandals.

The "bear scrape," so-called, was another event participated in by some members of Omega in common with many others. It was a more dangerous matter, involving no less serious an offense than the larceny of a live bear, and his subsequent killing and eating, a full account of which is given in another chapter.

III—SIGMA CHI, 1876–77.

It is not too much to say that the class of '77 contained the most energetic and zealous workers we ever had in the chapter. It had fourteen members, the largest number from any one class in Omega's history. During this year the example of Bro. Frank M. Elliot, and his businesslike attention to the chapter's interests, inspired all our actions. His spirit of loyalty and devotion, in dark times as well as bright, has saved the chapter when disasters came upon us, and the struggle seemed desperate. Such a splendid *morale*, which disappointments cannot impair, is in no sense natural or spontaneous. It is the outgrowth of discipline and moral training—the moral training which Omega gives her children in the code of honor of Sigma Chi. No other bond can unite students into so compact and coherent a body. When Greek meets Non-Greek in college life it is like the impact of veteran soldiers with the rabble. Numbers count for nothing against discipline, courage and devotion to the flag. The training which college fraternities thus give their members is of priceless value in afterlife. It gives them powers of organization, the ability to sway men and events. It teaches them the value of fidelity and practical trustworthiness, without which a large part of the world's business could not be done. It teaches the value of tact, courage and boldness.

Of the fourteen Sigs of '77, only Evans, Elliot, Early and Knappen graduated in that year. Demorest joined '78; he is now in the ministry.

Moss is an architect in Chicago. Baker graduated at Ann Arbor as a civil engineer. Martin L. Anderson, of this class, was shortly after graduation made a Sig; he became an instructor in the Lake View High School, and is now engaged in the cattle business in the West. W. G. Evans, the oldest son of Gov. Evans, one of the founders of Evanston, and of the Northwestern University, was an ardent promoter of public enterprises in the school, not only with his energy and business enterprise, but often with more than his share of money donated outright. Mention has been made of his name in connection with the gymnasium. He probably did more than any other student at the college to develop all athletic sports, and particularly baseball. He held the position of captain of the strongest nine the University ever had, and it was through long and careful gymnasium and out-door training under his rigid discipline that it became superior, probably, to any western amateur nine, certainly to the Elgin club, which was really half professional. The senior lecture and concert course, under Bro. Evans' management, was eminently successful that year, and the entertainments given were of a high order.

Of Albert D. Early, whom his intimate friends delighted to call Gee, the memory is lasting and pleasant. He is known to most of the later members, having kept up his old interest in Omega. Like the two men we have mentioned, he was hearty, whole-souled and generous,— the man above all others whom a brother could trust and fall back on in case of trouble.

We have already spoken of Frank E. Knappen. Like Evans, he was much addicted to baseball and athletics. An exploit of his was the cause of some difficulty with the faculty at one time. This was a desperate "Græco-Roman" wrestling match, which took place in the Adelphic Society hall, before a select audience. Care was taken by the college authorities that such a desecration did not occur in these premises again.

Evans is now in business in Denver, Colorado. Knappen and Early are lawyers in Kalamazoo, Michigan, and Rockford, Illinois, respectively. Elliot conducts a real estate business in Chicago. He now holds the position of Grand Annotator of the Sigma Chi Fraternity, and is one of the Triumvirs. Ezra B. Parrish, whose recent death is chronicled elsewhere, was a resident of Michigan. Earle Martin, another member of '77, who was absent during this year, is now in business in Chicago, a partner in Coffin, Devoe & Co. Morrison M. Gillet is a commercial traveler, with headquarters at Fond du Lac, Wisconsin.

IV — SIGMA CHI '77–78.

Omega, in the fall of '77, had four seniors,

including Demorest, who had joined the class from '77.

There was among all the fraternity men of the class the most cordial feeling and great unity of purpose, growing out of the fact that the anti-fraternity forces had combined and antagonized all members of secret fraternities from the very beginning. Whatever cliques had been formed in college elections outside of the class, the Greeks of '78 had never been guilty of any partisan work in class matters, and they felt indignant that they should be intrigued against as if they had done so.

They resolved that, since they were so discriminated against in class elections, they would show their mettle in all competition for honors, where merit alone decided.

The first struggle was for the Hurd prizes. Five were to be chosen from the class, the test being essays on a certain subject, handed in under an assumed name, so that merit alone should decide. The five best essays received prizes and their writers became the Kirk prize contestants.

Of these five honors Sigma Chi obtained three and Beta Theta Pi two. The fortunate men were Harris, Booth, Andrews, Ackerman and Kinman. Thus every Sig had a place, except Demorest, who made no effort.

Substantially the same state of affairs resulted

in the competition for places on commencement day. It became evident in the class meetings that the anti-fraternity members, who had steadily excluded fraternity men from elective places, were not well pleased with the latter's triumphs in these contests. A numerical majority of "bibs" and female students could outvote the society men, but could not compete with them on a basis of merit.

The determination they arrived at, as we soon became aware, was to put none but non-frats. in any of the positions to be chosen, viz.: classday speakers, class officers and important committees.

The principle avowed was that these places should be filled by those who had *not* already obtained other honors, in order to "give everyone a chance." In other words, the possession of one appointment was to deprive a member of his equal chance of obtaining another.

As about fifteen were in this position, classday places had to be filled from the remainder, and we knew what that would mean—a representation we would be ashamed of on class day.

We resolved simply to bolt with our camp followers, resign our membership in the class organization and refuse to appear on classday with its members so represented.

At the appointed time the election came off, and resulted even worse than we had feared. The most notoriously unfit persons were elected as historian, orator and poet; persons who on previous public occasions had made the class a laughing-stock. We at once offered our resignations and withdrew, constituting ourselves the "Solid Six," and took with us a few hangers-on of non-fraternity men. The "Solid Six' really numbered seven, namely, Harris, Booth, Andrews, of Sigma Chi; Haney, Hoag, Johnson, of Phi Kappa Sigma; Kinman, of Beta Theta Pi. Small as were our numbers, our influence was really great. We made no effort to injure the class organization after that, but calmly waited for them to hold their classday exercises, when we should be unable to attend on account of a private reception to our friends of Evanston held at the same hour.

The faculty was much disturbed over this quarrel, and proposed a "compromise," which was, that classday should be given up altogether. This was exactly the kind of a compromise we wanted, and we did not dissent. There was no classday in '78.

Our triumph in this case was not an example of "rule or ruin" disposition. We were simply determined not to remain in a class publicly represented by its worst members, but were perfectly willing that they should go on without us if they chose. When we found that the faculty was unwilling that there should be a classday unless we joined in it, we felt flattered by their esteem.

The "Solid Six" gave, on what would have been classday, a large reception to their numerous Evanston friends. The Social Club rooms were filled with light-hearted dancers until a late hour, and a keen pleasure was felt in being able to repay, in even a small degree, the generous hospitality of Evanston homes which had so added to the happiness of a four years' college course.

Another anti-fraternity struggle of some bitterness occurred that year in connection with the *Tripod*, the old college organ. This paper was owned and controlled by the Tripod Association, a joint meeting of the three literary societies, and was by them awarded to an editor-in-chief, who usually made a few hundred dollars in a year from it. Canvassing for the position of editor-in-chief was sometimes brisk, and this year Messrs. Haney and Andrews entered the field and were defeated by Ladd and Warrington for the editorship. The former had the backing of all the fraternity men, the latter of all the Biblical students, and much partisan feeling resulted.

It was finally determined by the two fraternity men not to rest under defeat, but to start a new periodical distinctively under the patronage of secret societies, and with one editor from each. Accordingly, Isaac E. Adams, of Beta Theta Pi; Conrad Haney, of Phi Kappa Sigma, and E. W. Andrews, of Sigma Chi, became the editors. They soon sent out circulars announcing that the *Vidette* would be issued semi-monthly, instead of monthly, as was its slow rival. Remarkable success attended the efforts to gain advertisements. Eight hundred dollars' worth were contracted for before the first issue.

By prompt action we "scooped" the *Tripod* completely, using the unanswerable argument that the "crowd" we represented were the students who spent all the money—for the "bibs" bought little or nothing except groceries for their clubs. No one cared to advertise books, jewelry, cigars or fine clothing in their paper, and these were the kind of advertisements which paid best. Another cause of trouble was the fact that they took their paper out of town to be printed, which set many local tradespeople against them.

The first issue of the *Tripod* demonstrated that it was in incompetent hands. Instead of being improved by competition it was a perfect botch,—in fact, the poorest for years, and full of typographical errors and misspelled words, being perfectly characteristic of its editor — Ladd, who was a hard student but an awful bungler with the English language. All this helped the

Vidette, which was modeled after the better Eastern journals and was moderately successful from a literary standpoint. Its chief ambition, however, was to become a mirror of student life and news, and in this respect its local editor, I. E. Adams, made it bright and interesting.

Subsequently the *Tripod* and *Vidette* were merged under the name *Northwestern*. The new paper became semi-monthly and adopted a heading and make-up almost a counterpart of those used in the *Vidette*. The latter may be said to have revolutionized college journalism at N. W. U.

W. H. Harris, a son of Bishop Harris, of the M. E. Church, was with '78 four years. He was awarded one half of the Kirk prize for best oration, and several other prizes in previous years.

Subsequently he attended Columbia Law School, and after graduation there, entered upon the practice of law in New York city, where he is now successfully engaged.

W. M. Booth likewise has followed the law. He was noted in college for his brilliancy in languages, especially Greek, which he mastered with great ease. For excellence in Greek he received a prize and also other honors, including the Hurd essay prize. Bro. Booth has always been a working Sigma Chi, and has helped to bear many of its burdens. As a member of the executive committee, which entertained the Grand Chapter at Chicago in 1882, he had to handle and disburse about $800, and, with Bros. Lunt and F. T. Andrews, bear a large amount of unrequited work. The success and éclat of that convention is largely due to his industry and ability. At present Bro. Booth is a member of the Grand Council and Triumvirs, being the Grand Quæstor of the Sigma Chi Fraternity, with headquarters at Chicago.

E. W. Andrews, after graduating, became a medical student and subsequently a surgeon. He is now living in Chicago. At the meeting of the Grand Chapter, in 1884, Bro. Andrews was elected Grand Prætor of the Fifth Province, and by virtue of his location in Chicago, was appointed one of the Triumvirs who perform the routine work for the Grand Council in governing the Sigma Chi Fraternity. Therefore we see three members of Omega, Bro. Elliot, of '77, and Bros. Booth and Andrews, of '78, in important positions in our new central government.

This is a high compliment to the chapter, which is so much younger and less deserving than many others. The location of its numerous alumni in the great metropolis, whither all eyes turn, is probably the true cause of the chapter having so much influence in the fraternity at large. The holding of the Grand Chapter at Chicago, in 1882, was also the means of making Omega widely known, and praised, perhaps, beyond her deserts. This event reacted most favorably upon the chapter by exciting in the members new zeal and new energy, as well as a better appreciation of the greatness and high standing of the fraternity as a whole.

E. WYLLYS ANDREWS.

CHAPTER XI.

FRATRES CAROS SALUTO.

Tune—"Lauriger Horatius."

Fratres caros saluto
   Vos, in aula nostra;
Crucem bene tuere,
   "In hoc signo vinces."

Chorus—Fratres voces tollite,
     Laudibus sonoris,
   Colentes pectoribus
     Sigma Chi aeterno.

Sunt beati juvenes,
   Qui advenant aram
Amatam a Sigma Chi,
   Cum amore vero.

Chorus—Fratres voces tollite, etc.

Unitate spargimur,
   Fratres, et "Sic esto;"
Ranaculus saluit
   Crocodili in tergum.

Chorus—Fratres voces tollite, etc.

D. E. Crozier.

CHAPTER XII.

OMEGA 1878–1879.

WITH the opening of the college year of 1878 and 1879 Omega found but seven names on her chapter-roll. The "Four Wills," Messrs. Booth, Andrews, Harris and Demorest, who had graduated in the June preceding, were sadly missed in the fall campaign. Two of the famous quartette, it is true, were often seen in their wonted haunts dropping words of wisdom which cheered the chapter in its loneliness. Perhaps it was a relief from severer studies to gather often round the council-board, for Andrews had entered the field of Æsculapius, and Booth, to use the very homely expression of Dr. Johnson, was "digging the bowels out of Blackstone." Another attraction grew out of a certain post-graduate compact entered into by these brothers, by which they were never allowed the luxury of a cigar save within the sacred shadow of their Alma Mater. But whatever the cause which drew them so frequently to Evanston, there was much rejoicing at their presence.

So it came about that the weakness of the chapter at this time was not apparent, though it was really the beginning of that period of depression experienced in the years following. With the active interest of recent alumni, and a chapter not strong, perhaps, but numbering some of the best men in college, the necessity for new members was forgotten. A cause which lay even deeper was depression in the University itself. The proportion of young men attending college was materially decreased by the hard times, and the institution laboring under a heavy debt, offered to students fewer attractions than in former years. The material from which to draw new members for the chapter lessened rapidly with this contraction in all departments of the University, and Omega felt that to lower her standard of requirement would be to accept defeat. Inanition was better than disgrace. In the two years following, this policy resulted in something of a struggle, but it was never regretted, for, with the general revival under the new *regime*, came an added life and energy.

Bros. Hesler and Owen were quietly initiated during the fall term and their names alone were added to the lists throughout the year. On November 19, at Indianapolis, convened the Tenth Biennial Session of the Grand Chapter, where Omega was represented by Bro. E. L. Stewart. Our chapter gained much through her admirable ambassador, in contemporary fraternity politics, and in her reputation throughout the order.

So the year came and went, and, if it be true that the annals of prosperity are short, this was a period of marked success. Though the depression of the next two years was soon to follow, no such result could be seen by the contemporary observer of events. The membership was suited to the best of social intercourse, and in size the chapter was well fitted for its object. The men composing it were of ability and standing. Five years have widely scattered those nine names. Lipps is a silk manufacturer in the south of France; Jessup is practicing medicine in New York; Andrews, Davis and Foulks follow the same profession in Chicago; Owen is seeking fortune in the Northwest; Donelson is connected with the Deering Machine Company; Stewart is a lawyer in Chicago; and Hesler is surgeon of the Flag Ship on the Atlantic Squadron.

* * *

CHAPTER XIII.

HISTORY OF OMEGA FROM SEPTEMBER, 1879, TO JUNE, 1884.

The glory of Omega had been gradually culminating since her reorganization until, during the years '77, '78 and '79, her preëminent superiority among the Greeks at Northwestern was admitted and recognized by all. With the return to college in the fall of '79 the brethren considered the prospects of the fraternity bright, and were happy and content to rest upon their laurels. We believe a more auspicious opening for a successful year has not been known in the history of the chapter. It is true that such men as were thought suitable for members of the Sigma Chi were more scarce than they had been heretofore. Yet there were some good men, and we secured all that were wanted. The names of Bross and Elliot, of '83, were soon added to our chapter roll, and, with this valuable acquisition of men who were greatly desired by the other fraternities, Omega prospered, and the spirit of satisfaction pervaded her halls.

During the year little work was done relative to the fraternity at large, and no minutes, unfortunately, of the regular meetings of the chapter were preserved. Yet it was a noticeable fact that the most zealous fraternity spirit existed among the brethren, and before the close of the year Kampf, '85; Tunnicliff, '84; De Groff, 81; Brown, '83, and Randolph, '81, were admitted into the mystic circle. The history of the chapter during this year is strongly characterized by the good fellowship which existed among the members. Being satisfied with our past record and the high reputation of our active members, we became to a certain degree indifferent to others and to the future, which were to supply the strength of the chapter when the present members should leave these classic shades for other fields of labor. Thus the collegiate year rolled on to the close, and four men from Sigma Chi graduated. This class was the first to complete its entire college course under the administration of Dr. Marcy, who was at that time the acting president. The class was certainly a credit to the institution, and well may the old doctor feel proud of it.

As it had been found impossible to relieve the University of its financial embarrassments, and owing to the necessary curtailment of expenses in advertising, and reducing the number of professors, the former reputation of the college before the public was not now fully sustained. Under these circumstances the opening of college in the fall of '80 found Omega Chapter with six men, Bros. Andrews, De Groff and Randolph, of '81; Elliot and Brown, of '83, and Tunnicliff, of '84. The freshman class was much smaller than any had been for many years, yet there was much good material in the class. The larger part of its members were quickly taken by the fraternities, many of whom joined or pledged themselves to secret societies before matriculating at the college.

On the evening of October 5, '80, Messrs. Geo. P. Merrick and A. D. Currier, both of '84, were ushered into the mystic circle of Sigma Chi. This being the first initiation of the year, a large number of the alumni brothers were present to give inspiration to the occasion, and to partake of the sumptuous "spread" to which they were invited. This event is particularly mentioned because on this occasion the first real action was taken toward establishing a chapter house for the use of Omega. The subject had long been considered by the active members of previous years, and it was now decided to lay the matter before our alumni. The result of this action was the appointment of a committee to take the matter in charge, and report as to the financial support of the enterprise. The subject was presented to all our members, soliciting their aid. In the meantime measures were taken to rent a building for our use until we should be able to establish one of our own. Thus, with bright hopes before us, we started out for a brilliant year. During the fall term H. L. Peck, '85, was initiated; so, with nine congenial souls, Omega was prosperous and happy. Bro. F. W. Randolph, '81, was the leading spirit this year in the chapter. He was a man of decided ability in literary and artistic pursuits, and a most loyal "Sig." He was untiring in his labors for the chapter, and the earnestness which he exhibited greatly inspired all his brothers.

This being the year for the Thirteenth Biennial Convention of Sigma Chi, Bro. R. V. De-Groff, '81, was chosen to represent Omega in the Grand Chapter, which was to meet at Washington, D. C. He was accompanied on his mission by Bro. F. T. Andrews, '81, and to the influence of these brothers is due many important measures which were then adopted; one of them being the decision to hold the next session of the Grand Chapter, in 1882, at Chicago, under the auspices of Omega chapter. The compilation of the fraternity history was also given to Omega. We were much pleased with the honor thus shown us by the fraternity, and we immediately began to lay our plans to execute the work before us. The winter term came and found us still in our old hall, the walls of which were profusely decorated with relics. Our own experiences were from time to time recorded by the artistic sketches of Bro. Randolph. Many were the "spreads" and jolly meetings, one of which was occasioned by the capture of the Beta Theta Pi turkey "Hyslops." Having several fine musicians, we never lacked that inspiration which good music always brings. During every meeting the old hall rang with jolly songs, and we venture to say that not one of the nine brothers can look back upon those good old times without the feeling of their being the brightest spots of life. Before the close of the year five of our brothers were obliged to leave the college on account of ill health. Bros. Andrews and DeGroff graduated this year. Bro. Randolph, who had been taking a course in the law school in connection with his regular collegiate studies, graduated with honors from the law department, and was only prevented from securing his diploma in the University by the technical interpretation of the rules by the faculty. The annual banquet was held at the Tremont House, and was one of the pleasantest occasions of the year.

At the opening of the college, in the fall of '81, Omega counted noses, and there were only two, Merrick and Currier. Bros. Randolph and Andrews retained their active membership and helped us in many substantial ways. The freshman class was greatly reduced, and only a few men were considered worthy of invitation to our chapter. These few men had been so filled with disparaging reports of the weak condition of our chapter, by our rival "frats," that they were loath to give a decision in our favor. Yet one did, Mr. Harry Lathrop, and he proved a most enthusiastic worker. Mr. F. M. Brewer also came in.

In November, assisted by the local alumni brethren, Omega gave a reception at the Avenue House. By this means our alumni were awakened to a more lively interest in the chapter, and our social standing was greatly increased. In fact, this reception was considered by all the greatest society event of the season. Thus our hopes increased. We improved our hall and everything was progressing smoothly. Before the close of the fall term, Bro. Randolph left for his new home at Lake Benton, Minn., where he was to practice law. Mr. H. C. Eddy, '86, was made a member, but he soon went to the Illinois Wesleyan University, at Bloomington, to finish his course, and there he was influential in having the present chapter of Sigma Chi established.

In the winter term of '81 and '82 we had only four men. The chapter-house scheme was abandoned for a time, and the compilation of the fraternity history was about all that engaged our attention. It was necessary, however, to have the co-operation of the various chapters in this matter, but they seemed to take no interest in it, and the result was we had no history to present at the next meeting of the Grand Chapter.

Omega kept up her standing in college and society, receiving more honors than any of our rival "frats," though constantly reviled and persecuted by some of them. They seemed to gloat over our reduced condition. In December the sad news came that Bro. Harry P. Brown was dead. He was greatly beloved by all for his manly character and his bright social qualities. A few months later there came another shock, which caused the deepest grief throughout the chapter. On the 11th day of March, '82, Bro. F. W. Randolph, who had recently left us with such bright hopes for the future, died and went to that better land above. This sudden death of one who was near and dear to us, and whose future promised to crown him with success and eminence, seemed to the chapter a cruel and crushing blow. Appropriate resolutions were passed, and the badge of mourning, which had scarcely been removed for Bro. Brown, was replaced. The Upsilon Chapter of the Phi Kappa Sigma Fraternity sent Omega a warm sympathetic letter of condolence. Their expressed sympathy at this most trying time was particularly grateful to us.

Bro. Lathrop left us to engage in business, and our active membership was reduced to three. Renewed efforts added W. T. Prime, '87, to our list, but he, too, soon left us. Bro. Merrick, in his felicitous chapter report to the Thirteenth Biennial Convention, aptly expressed our condition when he said, " the Omega chapter still continues to promenade down to the college halls under one umbrella."

When it was known at the annual banquet that Bro. Bross, who had already remained in the college a year simply on behalf of the chapter, and Bro. Merrick did not expect to return the coming year, the outlook seemed dubious. Yet the one member who was to return to represent Sigma Chi in Northwestern was greatly encouraged by the promised support of our resident alumni, who now understood the true condition of the chapter. Too much cannot be said in praise of the valiant efforts of these warm-hearted brethren, and especially are we indebted to Brothers Elliot, Hamline, Bross, Booth, F. T. and E. W. Andrews. Nothing can so inspire an undergraduate with loyal pride and love for his fraternity as the cheerful and active assistance of an alumnus. The hall was still retained by the single active member. All the offices were at his command. He could vote any measure up or down, and we have no doubt that this short and singular interregnum was entirely harmonious and peaceful.

The new men in college were thoroughly canvassed, and September 21, 1882, witnessed the first acquisition of a member. On top of this came the joyful news of Bro. Merrick's return. Our friends increased while our enemies grew more heartless. It was up-hill work, but victory at last perched upon our banner. On October 12, 1882, two of the men whom we desired cast their lot with Sigma Chi, much to the discomfort of our rivals; they were C. A. Wightman, '85, and Sidney Watson, '85; the former is the Grand Historian of the fraternity, and he has already honored us and himself by his able research into our past history, and collecting new material for its publication. On October 31, Frank B. Parkhurst, '87, joined our increasing and enthusiastic number. In a short time another sophomore, who has since proved a great prize for Sigma Chi, was induced to join our ranks—Mr. Charles S. Slichter became a member November 6.

The following day was the opening of the Thirteenth Biennial Convention, which took place at the Grand Pacific Hotel, at Chicago. Our brothers were all enthusiastic over this convention and zealously aided in making it one of the most successful in the history of the fraternity. Nothing gave Omega so much joy as to be able to report to that convention a chapter roll of seven men. The convention was not only a great benefit to our chapter, but it was the means of spreading the importance of the University more extensively. On the last day of the convention Omega made a signal victory. Hon. William Springer, a member of Beta Theta Pi, had sent his son, Ruter W. Springer, to Northwestern. No sooner was the fact known than the stalwarts of Omega cast their nets, and forthwith Mr. Ruter W. Springer became a Sigma Chi.

The day following the convention right proudly did we lead a delegation of one hundred visiting Sigma Chis, together with our alumni and active members, to the college building. Here we were all received most cordially by President Cummings, who volunteered the statement that the alumni of Sigma Chi in Northwestern were the men to whom the faculty pointed with pride as specimens of graduates of this institution. Being so boldly recognized and praised by the president, we naturally felt greatly encouraged.

The utmost harmony existed in the chapter. Good literary work was done, and to increase our efforts in this direction a cash prize of ten dollars was offered by Bros. Bross, Andrews and Booth for the best written essay. This prize was won by Bro.

Wightman. On February 2, 1883, our circle was increased by the admission of Mr. D. E. Crozier, whom we were proud to welcome in our midst, not only because of his wide reputation in musical circles, but because of his genial qualities as a true gentleman. Many improvements were made on our hall, making it the most attractive one in the village. The work accomplished in the first two terms of the collegiate year was enormous, and the results were gained by the united and persistent efforts of our brothers. Much is due to the assembly of the Grand Chapter, to the practical aid of our alumni, and not least of all, to two of the most loyal lady friends of Sigma Chi, Mrs. F. M. Elliot and Mrs. J. H. Hamline. Their efforts in our behalf were most hospitable and generous, and cannot be too highly appreciated.

Our next initiate was F. N. Clark, '87. Nothing further of importance occurred during the remainder of the collegiate year, except the establishment of Alpha Iota chapter at Bloomington, Illinois, through the agency of Omega. The annual banquet was held at the Union League rooms, and was largely attended. Among the alumni present was Bro. Frank E. Hesler; he was on his way home to seek and regain his health. His speech on the reminiscences of Omega will always be remembered; it was about the last utterance on fraternity matters he made. It was full of bright things, and carried us away with delightful and happy memories. On January 1, 1884, after a painful and lingering disease, he passed from this earth to his last sleep.

Omega had seven men at the opening of the college year, '83. She was strongly antagonized by all the other fraternities, but we succeeded in obtaining the prize man of the freshman class, Edwin L. Shuman, who was initiated October 25. In the winter term, Omega originated and carried out the scheme of holding a local convention of the Western chapters. The purpose was to discuss matters of general fraternal interest, and to become better acquainted with one another. The convention was held January 25 and 26, and delegates from eight chapters were represented. It was a grand success. The last evening of the convention was devoted to the Omega essay contest for the Elliot prize. All the active men contested except Bros. Watson and Crozier. The prize was awarded to Bro. Shuman. After the convention a banquet was given at the Avenue House. The delegates departed with the kindest of feeling, and looked hopefully to the time when they might meet again under as pleasant circumstances. One of the indirect results of this district convention was the establishment of a chapter at the University of Wisconsin at

Madison. This was worked up and perfected by an active member of Omega. The chapter was duly organized. The charter men went to Beloit, where Sigma Chi had a live and strong chapter, and received the necessary introduction to the goat. Bros. Elliot, Early and F. T. Andrews assisted materially in the formation of this chapter. On March 21, '84, Chas. Clapp became a member. The usual jolly time at such occasions brought out a large number.

The end of the collegiate year drew to a close, bringing with it the graduation of Bros. Currier and Merrick. They were the first men of Omega who had graduated since '81. Commencement week was the most important and brilliant that Northwestern has known. She celebrated her twenty-fifth anniversary. There was a large number of graduates present, and the alumni association was greatly strengthened. On the morning of alumni day a business meeting was held. The cause of the decline in the attendance to the University was warmly discussed. Bro. E. W. Andrews made himself famous by his bold stand in the defense of the University against the zealots of the Woman's College. In the afternoon a public entertainment was given. Bro. George L. Yaple, '72, was the orator. He was a member of the House of Representatives, being the first graduate from

Northwestern who had achieved that distinguished honor. His oration was scholarly, and delivered extempore in a clear and pleasant manner. The effort was justly considered one of the finest ever delivered at the institution. In the evening a grand banquet was given, in which the professors, trustees and alumni participated. Excellent music, a varied, well-cooked dinner, toasts and glees made up a fitting ending of the first twenty-five years' history of the Northwestern University. A. D. CURRIER.

CHAPTER XIV.

THE FOURTEENTH BIENNIAL CONVENTION ENTERTAINED BY OMEGA.

THAT it was the determination of the members of Omega Chapter to make the meeting of the Grand Chapter in November, 1882, a memorable and important one is illustrated by the following characteristic sentence in her chapter letter in the *Sigma Chi* of June, '82: "The legislation of this next convention will determine in a very marked degree what is to be the result of our present transition state, and where Sigma Chi is to take her stand among the great brotherhoods of America." The previous convention at Washington, D. C., in November, '80, while it partook of the general character of Sigma Chi conventions in maintaining an elaborate and meritorious literary program, together with profuse and delightful social entertainment and good fellowship, did also something else—it established the *Sigma Chi*. The foundation of this magazine marked the beginning of a change from one of the most conservative to one of the most progressive of American college fraternities, from one of the most secret to one of the most ready to let its light shine. It had been the work of this journal to prepare the order for the coming convention. It aroused the dormant energies. It refreshed and quickened every part. It gave a new unity and singleness of aim. It pointed out defects and demanded their remedy. Thus the delegates came to the Fourteenth Convention, as never before, fully acquainted with the necessities of the society and with the high purpose and courage to meet them. The work done by the convention consummated, in fact, a revolution in the entire policy of the fraternity. The government was radically changed from the unsteady and frequently inconsistent rule of a "parent" chapter to the firm and conservative control of an experienced body of responsible alumni. Sigma Chi has never enjoyed such wide-spread prosperity as since the adoption of her new form of government.

To tarry over measures which have brought such glory to Sigma Chi would indeed be pleasing, but we are to record *the means pursued by Omega* to make possible such brilliant results. Bros. Geo. Lunt, W. H. Booth and F. T. Andrews, all alumni, were selected by Omega as her committee of arrangements.

Early in May of '82 the committee met and drew up circulars calling on all Illinois Sigma Chis for the necessary funds to carry on the work. The response was both speedy and liberal, and nearly $800 were raised. To acquaint Sigma Chis everywhere with the fact of the convention, and to earnestly request their attendance, was the next step. Two thousand invitations, of tasty design, giving the names of the orator, poet and reception committee, were engraved and distributed. The Hon. John M. Hamilton, governor of Illinois, was chosen orator, and Hon. J. J. Piatt, poet. The palatial Grand Pacific Hotel was secured for the sessions of the Grand Chapter. The time for the meeting now drew on apace. Visitors and delegates began to arrive. On the evening of the 7th of November a party of about thirty visited the Grand Opera House and listened to "Patience." The delegates in a body occupied seats in the three rows just in front of the orchestra. A very pleasant surprise to all was the rendition on the part of the troupe of a very pretty improvised Sigma Chi song, which was, to be sure, right loyally applauded. Chicago never saw a jollier or merrier spectacle than when, on the next morning, about eighty of the brethren, mounted on the Tally-Ho coach, or seated in the six accompanying carriages, crossed over the river to the North side on a tour of inspection of Lincoln park and the elegant residences passed on the way. On the afternoon of the eighth the convention settled down to business in earnest, and did not rise from its labors till the business was fully completed, on the very eve of the banquet.

Thus many little diversions planned by the committee had to be foregone. The literary exercises of the Fourteenth Session of the Grand Chapter consisted in the masterly oration by Gov. Hamilton, and the poem of Bro. Piatt, which, in the latter's absence, was read by proxy. Immediately after occurred the banquet in the Ladies' Ordinary. There were about one hundred good and loyal Sigma Chis in attendance. Chaste and beautiful floral designs bearing the names of all the chapters represented were laid upon the plate of each delegate. The pleasure which these floral tokens seemed to inspire is one of the most pleasing remembrances of the committee. After the banquet came the toasts, with Hon. L. C. Collins as toastmaster. Witty, wise and beautiful were the responses. It was a late hour when, in reply to the last of the toasts, "the word which makes us linger," Bro. Merrick, '84, took his seat amidst a chorus of applause. The banquet and exercises were very agreeably interspersed with music by Freiberg's orchestra, which very acceptably rendered two Sigma Chi waltzes (by Bros. A. S. Kemp and Carl Merz, respectively), and a Sigma Chi Polka Mazurka (by E. H. Swen.) So ended the formal session of the Fourteenth Grand Chapter of Sigma Chi—the most reformative, the most improving and successful convention she has ever held. Still many of the delegates remained, and numerous were the pleasure excursions which followed the convention. Pullman, the most wonderful of industrial paradoxes, was visited. The stock-yards, packing-houses, and the engine-rooms of the Cable Car Company were inspected. The fire patrol gave an exhibition for their special benefit of its wonderful celerity in reaching a fire. Others embarked on the waters of Lake Michigan. On the morning of this last day of the Greeks' visit, seventy-five Sigma Chis took the cars for Evanston, and visited the Northwestern University, where they were very cordially received by the president, Joseph Cummings. His words in regard to the good influence of fraternities, and to the standing of Omega, are worthy of lasting preservation. We quote them entire:

"I have great pleasure in welcoming you this morning. I simply wish to say that as a college officer for many years at Middletown and other institutions, I have never entertained any of the feeling that sometimes exists with reference to fraternal organizations of this character. My associations with them have not been unprofitable.

"I have never found any difficulty arising therefrom; on the other hand, I have great pleasure in testifying that their influence is good. My own opinion is, that these associations maintain and intensify the sentiments of friendship and brotherly love. Most gentlemen who seek college education are men of high social character; the very influence you have in this association tends to strengthen this character, help the weak and foster the deserving. I have very favorable opinions of your fraternity. We are trying in this institution to do noble work; we are trying to make good and honorable men, as the name Illinois signifies, I believe. *I have great pleasure in saying that the men of this fraternity who have graduated from this institution are the men to whom we point with pride as specimens.* We shall always be happy if the men who go forth in the future are as good as these."

C. A. Wightman.

CHAPTER XV.

THE NORTHWESTERN DISTRICT CONVENTION OF SIGMA CHI.

ONE of the features of the college year of '83-'84, in fraternity circles, at Northwestern University, was the coming together, on January 25, '84, of the northwestern chapters of Sigma Chi in a district convention, for the twofold purpose of discussing fraternity work and plans and prospects and of extending and cementing friendly and fraternal intercourse among the chapters in the vicinity of Chicago. The idea was a new one and something in the nature of an innovation. Prior to this date there had been no meetings of the chapters of Sigma Chi, except at the regular biennial sessions of the Grand Chapter, and the meeting at Evanston was planned and called for the purpose of ascertaining the standing of the chapters in the Northwest, their views upon the various questions of fraternity policy, their attitudes concerning proposed plans, and, of no less importance, the creating of a more intimate relationship among contiguous chapters. It is not definitely known whose fertile brain it was that suggested the convention, but there are very strong suspicions that the honor lies between the well-known member of the general fraternity whose intelligence is recognized as among the best on fraternity matters, and the reserved and studious compiler of fraternity statistics and erstwhile admirer of his compeer "the magazine editor." But be that as it may, the convention was held, and all the Greeks wondered. Indiana was fully and ably represented by a goodly number of "typical Indiana Sigs," viz.: McMahon and Collins, of Xi; Fisher and Wiggam, of Chi, and Bro. C. W. Dawson, of Fort Wayne,—an old veteran Sig from Theta. Iowa sent from across the Mississippi Bro. Parker Holbrook, of Alpha Eta, and in him suffered nothing in influence, since his engaging manner and quiet, manly presence gained him attention, respect and consideration. Alpha Zeta, being at that time the only chapter in Wisconsin, sent as her delegates Bros. Bliss and Cleveland, the one taking the role of *raconteur celebre*, the other the difficult task of attracting the attention of the "chair." Of course Illinois was on hand. To say nothing of Evanston and Chicago, Heath of Kappa Kappa, and Ader, "Adipose Ader," and Stahl from Alpha Iota, at Bloomington, contributed not a little to confirm the prevalent but nevertheless mistaken impression that Illinois men are very wont to occupy the floor.

It will not be questioned, I take it, that the old halls of Omega never contained so many brilliant ideas all ready to blossom forth as at that time, and it is also a fact beyond all possibility of dispute that the aforesaid ideas found eloquent though not always uninterrupted expression. The latter adjective is imperative here, because of the numerous points of order raised by Omega's astute parliamentarian and true son of his father.

Despite the warnings of the now deposed grand councilman that the convention was encroaching upon the exclusive rights of the eminent board of which he formed a part, and constant reminders from the same source that "we should not transgress our authority," the convention progressed swimmingly. The magazine was subjected to a close examination; fraternity extension was lauded by one and berated by another; the song-book was laughed at, prayed for and wept over; rival fraternities were not neglected by any means, though by general consent deemed unworthy of serious attention. As a result the convention after two days and two nights' session made a lengthy and detailed report, recommending the Grand Chapter to take action upon many propositions, which were, in fact, adopted at the convention in the following August.

It is perhaps not essential here to give a digest

of the report, as it was made only in the form of a recommendation, but suffice it to say that the discussions and the action taken at that time had very much to do in improving the mode of fraternity government, which was made a prominent feature at the convention in Cincinnati.

At one of the evening sessions the Omega undergraduates read essays in competition for the Elliot prize—a prize given by Bro. Frank M. Elliot, of Omega, and established by him. The evening was pleasantly and no doubt profitably spent, the essays being written upon a fraternity topic and of interest to all Sigma Chis. Much to the surprise of all, the best essay was the production of the "infant" member and a freshman, though seniors, juniors and sophomores competed. Bro. Edward L. Shuman was awarded the prize and received the deserved congratulations of his auditors.

The convention closed its session on the afternoon of the 26th of January, and in the evening a supper was given by Omega to the "visiting statesmen." After an attenuated discussion of the *dishes* for which the Avenue House is noted, Dr. Andrews, of Omega, delivered an address of welcome, and proposed the following toasts:

The Local Convention . . Parker Holbrook, Alpha Eta.
Our Magazine . . . W. L. Fisher, Chi.
The Iron Clad Oath . . . W. A. Heath, Kappa Kappa,

Ye Old Sigs	C. M. Dawson, Theta.
Our Rivals	F. D. Ader, Alpha Iota.
The Goat	C. M. Bliss, Alpha Zeta.
"Indiana Sigs"	E. W. McMahon, Xi.
Chicago Alumni	F. M. Elliot, Omega.

All of the toasts were happily responded to and much merriment and good feeling prevailed. At a late hour the fraternal company dispersed, voting the district convention a grand success and, in the terse vocabulary of Oliver Twist, calling for "more." G. P. MERRICK.

CHAPTER XVI.

PRIZE MEN OF OMEGA.

Lorin C. Collins, '72; Day prize for best essay in competition for place on Blanchard contest.

George Lunt, '72; Day prize for best essay in competition for place on Blanchard contest.

Edwin J. Harrison, '72; Day prize for best essay in competition for place on Blanchard contest.

Merritt C. Bragdon, '71; Adelphic Declamation contest, second prize.

Clarence R. Paul, '72; Lunt prize for best dissertation on classical and English philosophy.

Henry Allen Cooper, '73; Junior prize, June 7, '72. Debate prize between junior and sophomore classes. Hurd prize for best essay in competition for place on Blanchard contest. Blanchard prize, one-half prize, for best oration.

William M. Knox, '74; Lunt prize for best English essay. Hurd prize for best essay on scientific subject.

John Henry Hamline, '75; Hurd prize for best essay in competition for place on Blanchard contest.

Frank Mitchell Harris, '75; prize in Descriptive Geometry.

Fred M. Taylor, '76; Sophomore Debate prize

for best debate between junior and sophomore classes, June 19, '74. Hurd prize in competition for place on Easter contest. Easter prize, one-half, for writing and pronouncing the best English oration. Intercollegiate prize for best English essay in contest at New York, '76. Intercollegiate prize, second prize, for excellence in mental philosophy, in contest at New York, 1876.

Winfield Scott Mathew, '76; Preparatory declamation prize, June 10, '70. Kedzie prize, second prize, for best freshman declamation, March 6, '73. Hurd prize for best essay in competition for place on Easter contest. Easter prize, one-half, for writing and pronouncing the best English oration.

Theophilus B. Hilton, '76; Gage prize for excellence in debate, March 19, '75.

Charles P. Wheeler, '76; silver-mounted rosewood base-ball bat for highest average batting during season '76.

Frank E. Knappen, '77; Sophomore contest prize for best declamation between junior and sophomore classes, February 9, '75. Gage prize for excellence in debate, January 18, '76.

Henry Frank, '77; Kedzie prize for best freshman declamation, March 9, '74.

Frank M. Elliot, '77; Hurd prize for best essay in competition for place on Easter contest.

William H. Harris, '78; Phillips prize for excellence in English composition, 1875. Rock River Seminary prize for excellence in Latin scholarship during sophomore year, 1876. Deering prize for best essay in competition for place on Kirk contest. Kirk prize, one-half, for writing and pronouncing best English oration.

William M. Booth, '78; Kedzie prize for excellence in Greek scholarship. Deering prize for best essay in competition for place on Kirk contest.

Edward Wyllys Andrews, '78; Deering prize for best essay in competition for place on Kirk contest Valedictorian class, '81, Chicago Medical College.

Nathan S. Davis, Jr., '80; Hinman prize for best English essay, 1878. Edwards prize for best scholarship record in College of Medicine (undergraduate), 1882. Faculty prize for thesis representing the best original investigation, 1883. Alumni prize for best scholarship record, 1883, all classes competing in College of Medicine.

George Peck Merrick, '84; Gage prize, second prize, for excellence in debate, 1882. Deering prize for best essay in competition for place on Kirk contest.

Charles A. Wightman, '85; Omega Alumni essay prize, 1883.

Edwin L. Shuman, '87; Scholarship at Northwestern University for entire course, for highest grade in examinations at entering college, 1883. Elliot prize for best English essay, 1884.

Total prize men, twenty-three; total prizes, forty-four.

Omega Speakers on Commencement.

F. C. Winslow, 1870.
A. D. Langworthy, 1870.
M. C. Bragdon, 1870.
George L. Yaple, 1871.
Hamilton S. Wicks, 1871.
Lorin C. Collins, 1872.
James G. Burke, 1872.
Eltinge Elmore, 1872.
E. H. Beal, 1872.
George E. Bragdon, 1872.
Edwin J. Harrison, 1872.
Frederick D. Raymond, 1872.
C. R. Paul (excused), 1872.
J. Frank Robinson, 1872.
Henry A. Cooper, 1873.
Theophilus B. Hilton, 1876.
Winfield Scott Mathew, 1876.
William G. Evans, 1877.
Frank E. Knappen, 1877.
William M. Booth, 1878.
W. L. Demorest, 1878.
William H. Harris, 1878.

Dexter P. Donelson, 1879.
C. A. Foulks, 1880.
Robert B. Jessup, 1880.
Nathan S. Davis, Jr., 1880.
Mason Bross, 1884, law college.
Albert D. Currier, 1884.
   Total, twenty-eight.

Omega Class-Day Orators.

Hamilton S. Wicks, 1871.
Henry A. Cooper, 1873.
Winfield Scott Mathew, 1876.
Albert D. Currier, 1884.

Washington's Birthday Orators.

George L. Yaple, 1871.
James S. Norris, 1875.

Lincoln's Birthday Orators.

Winfield Scott Mathew, 1875.
Fred M. Taylor, 1875.

Omega Orators Before the Alumni Association.

Hamilton S. Wicks, 1875.
George L. Yaple, 1884.

Men of Omega who appeared on Junior Class Exhibitions.

F. C. Winslow, March 23, 1869.
A. D. Langworthy, March 23, 1869.

M C. Bragdon, March 23, 1869.
J. F. Robinson, March 28, 1871.
C. R. Paul, March 28, 1871.
George Lunt, March 28, 1871.
J. G. Burke, March 28, 1871.
George E. Bragdon, March 28, 1871.
E. H. Beal, March 28, 1871.
Henry A. Cooper, May 3, 1872.
John H. Hamline, March 26, 1874.
Fred M. Taylor, March 24, 1875.
A. S. Appleton, March 24, 1875.
W. S. Mathew, March 24, 1875.
Frank E. Knappen, March 23, 1876.
E. W. Andrews, March 19, 1877.
W. M. Booth, March 19, 1877.
W. H. Harris, March 19, 1877.

These exhibitions were discontinued by the faculty after this date. The first exhibition took place April 6, 1859.

Men of Omega who appeared on Hinman Essay Contests.

William M. Knox, February 9, 1874.
John H. Hamline, March 12, 1875.
J. S. Norris, March 12, 1875.
Frank E. Knappen, May 4, 1877.
W. H. Harris, May 16, 1878.
E. W. Andrews, May 16, 1878.
Nathan S. Davis, Jr., May 9, 1879. Prize.

Raymond V. De Groff, May 20, 1881.
George P. Merrick, April 20, 1883.

Men of Omega who appeared on Junior and Sophomore Declamation Contests.

Daniel C. Riehl, May 20, 1873.
John H. Hamline, May 19, 1874.
A. S. Appleton, May 19, 1874.
Frank E. Knappen, February 9, 1875.
F. M. Taylor, February 9, 1875.
W. L. Demorest, January 13, 1876.
W. M. Booth, January 13, 1876.
George P. Merrick, April 7, 1882.

Men of Omega who appeared on Junior and Sophomore Debate Contests.

Henry A. Cooper, June 7, 1872. Prize.
Fred M. Taylor, June 19, 1874. Prize.
T. B. Hilton, Jr., March 19, 1875. Prize.
Frank E. Knappen, January 18, 1876. Prize.
George P. Merrick, April 6, 1882. Second prize.
Albert D. Currier, April 6, 1883.
Charles A. Wightman, March 24, 1884.

Omega as Represented on Freshman Declamation Contests.

I. E. Lambert, March 8, 1872.
F. M. Taylor, March 6, 1873.
W. S. Mathew, March 6, 1873. Second prize.
W. L. Demorest, March 9, 1874.

F. E. Knappen, March 9, 1874.
A. D. Early, March 9, 1874.
Henry Frank, March 9, 1874. First prize.
F. A. Early, March 9, 1874.
These contests were discontinued after this latter date by the faculty.

Men of Omega who have appeared on Contests and Public Entertainments, or occupied honorable positions not mentioned elsewhere in these annals.

Henry A. Pearson, trustee of N.W. U., 1882–1885.

George L. Yaple, poet of his class, 1871.

Eltinge Elmore, president of class, 1872.

James G. Burke, historian of class, 1872.

F. D. Raymond, memorialist of class, 1872.

C. R. Paul, ivy orator of class, 1872.

L. C. Collins, captain life-boat of class, 1872.

F. M. Taylor, chorister of class, 1876; debater friendly contest of literary societies, November 6, 1874.

T. B. Hilton, jr., orator burning books, 1876; debater friendly contest of literary societies, November 6, 1874.

W. S. Mathew, ivy orator, 1876.

F. E. Knappen, declamation, March 21, 1873, joint session literary societies.

F. A. Early, editor, March 21, 1873, joint session literary societies.

F. M. Harris, thesis; college of technology.

James E. Deering, speaker Euphronian anniversary, February 18, 1876.

Henry Frank, speaker friendly contest, Tri Kappa and Hinman, October 1, 1873; prize at Harvard College.

John W. Bennett, speaker Preparatory anniversary, June 17, 1876.

W. M. Knox, orator literary entertainment, February 26, 1874; orator friendly contest of Tri Kappa and Hinman, at Chicago, December 11, 1873; subject, 12 to 1.

J. S. Norris, declamation literary entertainment, February 26, 1874; orator friendly contest literary societies, November 6, 1874.

F. W. Randolph, essayist Public School, June 26, 1874; prophet class, 1881; prize oration Union College of Law, 1881.

M. M. Gillet, debater entertainment December 13, 1872.

E. B. Parrish, debater entertainment December 13, 1872.

W. G. Evans, president, class 1877.

Frank M. Elliot, secretary and treasurer Alumni Association, 1883-1884; President Alumni Association, 1884-1885; Grand Aannotator Sigma Chi Fraternity, 1884-1886.

W. H. Harris, declamation joint session literary societies, December 15, 1876; editor joint session literary societies, winter 1878.

George P. Merrick, orator joint session literary societies, February 16, 1883; Grand Quæstor Sigma Chi Fraternity, 1882–1884.

E. W. Andrews, responsive address on behalf of class '81, Chicago Medical College; Grand Prætor fifth province Sigma Chi Fraternity, 1884–1886.

W. M. Booth, Grand Quæstor Sigma Chi Fraternity, 1884–1886.

Booth, Andrews, Elliot, Grand Triumvirs Sigma Chi Fraternity, 1884–1886.

A. D. Currier, orator open session Hinman, October 14, 1882.

R. V. Jessup, Jr., president class, 1880.

Charles S. Slichter, president class, 1885.

C. A. Wightman, essayist open session Hinman, November 9, 1883; Grand Historian Sigma Chi Fraternity, 1884–1886.

It will be observed, from an examination of these several lists, that over one half of the men of Omega are represented in them. It is well to bear in mind, in this connection, that a number of the members did not graduate, and had, therefore, no opportunity of appearing on contests and public programmes.

CHAPTER XVII.

THE BLANCHARD PRIZE.

One of the oldest and most important prizes offered for competition in the University is the Blanchard. The honor of establishing this meritorious prize is due to Mr. R. P. Blanchard, of the class of '70. It was his intention to endow it with the sum of one thousand dollars, the interest of which would aggregate one hundred dollars, and this was to constitute an annual prize. This, however, was not done, and Mr. Blanchard paid, instead, the hundred dollars each year until 1876, when financial difficulties overcame him. The prize known as "The Blanchard" ceased at that time. One of the generous citizens of Evanston, Mrs. J. D. Easter, then donated the required amount, and the prize was known as "The Easter." In 1878 another change took place, and the money for the prize was kindly given by Mrs. James S. Kirk. Since this latter change the prize has been called "The Kirk."

The prize, as already stated, is one hundred dollars, and is given to that member of the senior class who shall write and deliver the best English oration. In order to compete for this prize the contestant must be free from conditions. The number of competitors is five, and they are selected by the faculty after examining their essays. The subjects for the essays are given out by the faculty about a year before the oratorical contest takes place. The essays are sent in to compete for a prize established as the "Day" prize, and which was changed in '73 to the "Hurd" prize. It was again changed in '78 to "The Deering" essay prize. The five persons who write the best essays receive ten dollars each and are entitled to appear in the oratorical contest. Instead of dividing the Hurd prize, it was given entirely to the one who wrote the best essay.

The oratorical prize is looked forward to by a large number of students with anxious eyes, as the most desirable thing to obtain while in college. A diploma is of little consequence in comparison with this honor. To win the Blanchard, the Easter, or the Kirk, is worth all the other gifts of the institution put together. It is considered a high privilege to compete for this prize, and the goal of the student's ambition in college is reached when he has won it.

The Blanchard was inaugurated by the class of '71, and the first contest took place June 23 of that year. The managers of the prize adopted a new feature for commencement exercises, and introduced the custom of charging an admittance fee. The reasons set forth by the contestants for adopting this course sound strange enough to this later generation, but were no doubt valid and sufficient for that time. They were as follows: "First, To debar the little boys who invariably disturb the exercises. Second, Without some distinction of this kind we cannot provide for seating comfortably those who would like to attend for the purpose of hearing the speeches and music. Third, By the additional help of twenty-five cents from each spectator we shall be able to provide *first*-class music. Fourth. It will scarcely be expected that four individuals could afford to expend $80 or $100 in the way of *first*-class music, programs, hall rent, elocutionary drill, etc., for the public, when only one can possibly receive any financial remuneration in return; besides, at other colleges it is customary to have one entertainment the proceeds of which are applied to help defray necessary expenses." The expenses of this contest are now paid by the University. The first contest was presided over by Dr. E. O. Haven, then president of the University.

The following is a complete list of the contestants for the different years, the names of the prize winners, and their subjects:

1871.—J. H. Raymond, E. R. Shrader, R. D. Russell, H. W. Woodruff, C. W. Pearson, excused.

Prize divided between Raymond, whose subject was, "The Permanence of Our National Institutions," and Shrader, whose subject was "Edwin M. Stanton."

1872.—Lorin C. Collins, George Lunt, R. B. Edwards, E. J. Harrison, W. O. Peet, A. L. Smith. Prize given to Smith; subject, "Cavour and Italy." The judges found the essays so even in merit that six men were allowed to appear on the contest.

1873.—Henry A. Cooper, E. C. Arnold, F. W. Cleveland, J. R. Leslie, Henry Green. Prize divided. Cooper; subject, "The Third Napoleon and the Lessons of His Career." Arnold; subject, "Unification of Mankind."

1874.—William M. Knox, W. L. McGarry, Eli McClish, R. G. Hobbs, M. S. Kaufman. Prize divided. McClish; subject, "The Jew." Arnold; subject, "Charles Sumner."

1875—John H. Hamline, F. M. Warrington, J. J. Crist, J. F. Stout, F. A. Hills. Prize given to Crist; subject, "Oliver Cromwell."

1876—Easter Prize: F. M. Taylor, F. H. Scott, W. S. Mathew, S. S. Bradford, S. C. McPherrin. Prize divided. Taylor; subject, "Napoleon Bonaparte." Mathew; subject, "Lincoln and Slavery."

1877—C. H. Morgan, E. J. Bickell, H. R. Antes, Elizabeth R. Hunt, Frank M. Elliot. Prize given to Morgan; subject, "The Moral Element in Human Progress"; honorable mention, Miss Hunt.

1878—W. M. Booth, E. W. Andrews, W. H. Harris, E. M. Kinman, W. M. Ackerman. Prize divided. Harris; subject, "The Duty of the Scholar in American Politics." Ackerman; subject, "The Search for Truth."

1879—T. H. Hood, W. A. Hamilton, J. T. Musgrove, Jessie Moore, Ella S. Prindle. Prize given to Miss Moore; subject, "The Wesleyan Reformation."

1880—F. A. Wood, W. B. Norton, Helen L. Miller, Cassie M. Scott, Julia D. Watson. Prize won by Miss Watson; subject, "The Scottish Covenanters."

1881—George A. Foster, P. H. Swift, W. H. Huston, J. P. Brushingham, J. A. Matlack. Prize given to Foster; subject, "The Epic Period of American History."

1882—F. H. Sheets, Frank M. Merrill, H. H. Miller, Emily Hatfield, Emma Prindle. Prize given to Miss Prindle; subject, "Edmund Burke."

1883—J. C. Bannister, M. M. Gridley, H. H. Denman, J. T. Hatfield, W. E. Wilkinson. Prize given to Bannister; subject, "Hildebrande."

1884—George P. Merrick, C. S. Raddin, W. F. Atchison, W. H. Crawford, Charles Horswell. Prize given to Crawford; subject, "William the Silent."

There have been thirteen Sigma Chis on these contests during the period of fourteen years. She has won one-half of four prizes. Ten of the subjects of the winners were biographical; four, historical; three, abstract-religious, and two, abstract-political.

CHAPTER XVIII.

MISCELLANY—THE SPADE AND SERPENT.

To the class of '75 is due the credit of establishing a class secret society, modeled after those at Harvard and Yale. The object was to create a higher scholarship and bring into closer relations members of the same class, who had previously been held apart by membership in the ordinary secret societies. The plan was to select not more than fifteen men from the incoming senior class who were recognized as being more than ordinary students, and to make the society so attractive and select that from the freshmen to the senior year the student would prepare himself to become entitled to membership in it. The society was organized in the spring of 1875, and was called the Spade and Serpent. It adopted a badge in the form and appearance of a miniature coffin, made of gold and black enamel, bearing on its face, in gold relief, a spade, around which was entwined a serpent.

It started with fifteen men, the principal movers being J. H. Hamline, L. C. Coleman, F. M. Warrington, J. J. Crist, and A. R. Robinson.

During commencement of 1875 the society elected from the incoming class A. S. Appleton,

F. M. Taylor, J. W. Dickson, T. B. Hilton, Jr., J. A. J. Whipple, W. S. Mathew, F. H. Scott, C. P. Wheeler, C. A. Gardner and A. W. McPherson. The society offered a junior prize of $25, to be given to that member of the junior class who should attain the highest scholarship. The faculty, however, refused to award it, as it did not wish in this public manner to recognize secret societies.

Although the society was of great benefit to the class of '75 in bringing into closer relations the members who had formerly been somewhat noted for their lack of interest in one another, still it did not possess the vitality necessary for a long existence. The Spade and Serpent Society did not live long, but before its final dissolution it very properly gave and bequeathed the $25 refused by the faculty to the alumni association.

THE LIFE-SAVING CREW.

After the wreck of the Lady Elgin, in August, 1860, and the terrible loss of life by that noted disaster, the government authorities at Washington were solicited to establish a life-saving station here. The matter rested for a long time, until October 1, 1871, when a life-saving boat was presented to the University by the government. The crew which manned this boat was taken from the students in college, and generally from the senior class. It became a custom on class-day to present the boat to the incoming senior class. The first crew consisted of L. C. Collins, coxswain; George Lunt, stroke; E. J. Harrison, bow; Eltinge Elmore, George Bragdon, F. Roys and M. D. Kimball.

It was largely through the efforts of the class of '72 that the life-boat was secured, and it is from this beginning that has grown the artistic and useful building which adorns our campus on the lake shore. It is considered one of the most important and best equipped government stations on the Great Lakes.

THE FAMOUS NINE OF 1871.

One of the most famous baseball nines ever in the University played during the season of 1871. It was the time when high scores were made, and when the contests were most spirited. The nine was composed of the following men: Kimball, c.; Langworthy, s.s.; Collins, p.; Gains, 1b.; Lunt, 2b.; Drake, 3b.; Beaty, r.f.; Elmore, c.f.; Cooper, l.f.; Simmons, scorer.

During the season the nine played thirteen games and lost only two. It defeated the famous White Stocking Club, of Chicago, on June 3, 1871, by a score of 18 to 12. The usual scores made were enormous. The lowest was 11 and the highest 68. There was one of 57, one of 43, another 39 and one 35. Six of the nine were Sigma Chis.

THE VELVET-TOPS.

A club called the Velvet-Tops was organized with the object in view of having meals properly selected and cooked at a reasonable price. Simon Peter Douthart was the steward, and he did his part in a satisfactory manner. It started in January, 1877, and continued for several months, until the price of membership became so high that it was necessary to disband it. The Velvet-Tops were not delicate eaters, by any means; they consumed four hundred pounds of beef in the last two weeks of the club's existence, to say nothing of the other items on the bill of fare. Nearly all of the active Sigma Chis were members of this famous club.

KING KALAKUA.

When King Kalakua, of the Sandwich Islands, was visiting this country in 1875, it occurred to some of our missionary brothers that it would be a good idea to make him an honorary member of the fraternity. It was said that when Prince Albert was in the country on a visit, he was made a member of a college fraternity at Cornell, and he was so pleased and gratified by the distinguished honor conferred upon him, that upon his return to his home he purchased an elegant library of one thousand volumes and sent it to the chapter which had made him a member. Whether this was the motive for attempting to make King Kalakua a Sigma Chi is not known; at any rate, a profound document was issued, with all the pomposity of the Knights of the Crusades, and sent to his excellency at Chicago. It informed his royal highness that he had been made a member of our mystical association, and owing to his high and honorable career as a statesman and a philanthropist, the form of initiation would be modified in his case, and that all that would be required of him would be to pay the customary initiation fee of $500. This distinguished nabob, the king of the Cannibal Islanders, was not civilized enough to even acknowledge the receipt of this communication, but passed us by and went to Milwaukee, when he had the thirty-third degree of the masonic order conferred upon him, and for which he afterward set up the beer.

WOOGLIN AND HIS DORG.

In the fall of 1875 Mr. David Cavan, the genial and accomplished editor of the *Index*, was short of copy for his paper. He mentioned the fact to a student friend, whereupon the friend said that he had a story at home which he thought would do credit to his paper and be of especial interest to the students. "Just the thing," replied Mr. Cavan, "bring it in, by all means, and I will publish it." The following issue of the *Index* contained the story. It was read with decided relish by all the students, except the Beta Theta Pi members. They regarded it as extremely unfortunate, and could express their high dudgeon in no stronger terms than "scorning" those who were supposed to have been instrumental in having it published. The story was a statement of the secret tenets of their fraternity, giving a full and accurate account of Wooglin and his Dorg. For a long time after the "eye of Wooglin" was of a deep vermilion hue, indicating, it was believed, intense disgust and anger. The "dorg" departed from its mythical nature and assumed the attitude of its prototype when its feelings are hurt, and has since appeared with its tail more or less crooked between its legs.

THE GREEKS AT NORTHWESTERN.

PHI KAPPA PSI.—Alpha chapter, of Illinois, founded in 1864. The chapter was suspended in 1870, and remained in this condition until reorganized, May 25, 1878. Total membership, 101.

SIGMA CHI.—Omega chapter was established in June, 1869. Its total membership to date, 110.

PHI KAPPA SIGMA.—Upsilon chapter was founded in 1872. Total membership, 75.

BETA THETA PI.—Rho chapter was established in July, 1873. Total membership, 69.

DELTA UPSILON (non-secret).—Northwestern chapter was established February 18, 1880. Total membership, 42.

CHAPTER XIX.

I — FRATERNITY INFLUENCE.

COLLEGE secret societies are no longer an experiment. They have been thoroughly tried, and their success and progress have been marked as popular and beneficent. It is a fact now believed by the foremost educators in the United States that, properly managed, and inspired by correct principles, they are an immense power for good.

The influence of a fraternity is second to none in the experience of a student's college life. The time of entering college is the receptive period. During the four years the student will receive more than he will give out, and the things received, the discipline of the mind, and the cultivation of the heart, will abide longer and be more potent in the formation of character than impressions received during any other similar period. The mastery of the curriculum of a college is the present and absorbing object, the ulterior object being a happy and successful progress through life, usefulness to mankind and a consciousness of having done well.

Very closely allied to this mental progress should be, and is to a large extent, the social progress, or the cultivation of the heart. And just here the college fraternity steps in and claims the honor of promoting this heart culture, which binds its members with those ties of friendship and love which are more lasting than any other outside of the family circle. To be in a class for four years does not hold or cement friendships as does the influence of a college fraternity. How to extract roots and formulate equations is what the Professors insist we shall know, and what they hope we shall remember to our dying day. But how soon are all these forgotten! Quite different are the things connected with a fraternity. How we delight in calling to mind the pleasures which its associations have given us, and how earnest its members are in promoting the general welfare of the fraternity!

Too much stress cannot be laid on the influence of a college fraternity. It has in its power the destiny of young men. Its influence may be of the greatest benefit, or, if not properly directed, it may become very pernicious. On this account too much care cannot be exercised in admitting only proper members. The conduct of the men should be recognized as pure and upright, whether in college, in the chapter hall, or in the business world. Everything that is of good report should be around the chapter, and everything should be done to make it as enduring as the University itself.

The Northwestern University has passed its first twenty-five years. Its trials are mostly over. Its pioneer work is finished. Its future is great, and there is every reason to believe that it will continue down the ages of time as the leading institution of learning in this great center. Its immense land interests and endowments, so prudently and wisely secured, prevent it from ever being overthrown by the whims of trade or by the convulsions of a panic. Nothing but a foreign invasion, or the act of God, will be able to unseat the Northwestern University. In view of these facts, nothing can be more important for Omega than to lay firm her foundations. With the prestige of fifteen years of a ripe and vigorous organization; a time filled with many successes and cherished honors; with the strength of its members—men who are fast reaping the rewards of a good and courageous life; with a character sustained by noble principles, and a wise policy pervading its government, there is little more now to be done to give Omega the rich and deserving legacy of a thousand years' life. Her principles are those which will live as long as truth and virtue exist; and her membership is sufficiently large and important to honor her in name, and to excite the highest aspirations among her younger members.

II — OMEGA CHAPTER HOUSE.

It has been pleasant for a number of our brothers to think of Omega for a long time as domiciled in a home of her own. These friends, whose faith in this enterprise is fortified with substantial backing, have organized *The Omega Chapter Home Association* under the laws of Illinois. The members of the board of directors are: Merritt C. Bragdon, Henry A. Pearson, John H. Hamline, James E. Deering and Frank M. Elliot. A house is desired which will contain all the attractions of a well regulated home. There should be, it is thought by these brothers, an open, recognized attraction in it, such as a large, well-lighted reading room with all the current literature on its tables—literature which shall embrace all the available secret-society publications, the best recognized scientific, educational and religious magazines, and the best daily, weekly and illustrated papers—the nucleus of a chapter library, to be increased, and to comprise a large, well assorted, miscellaneous class of books suitable for students, to be used as text and reference books, and such other works that will stimulate their minds and make the chapter house a pleasant and inviting retreat from the idle and promiscuous throng outside. This being a distinctive feature, the other accessories of a secret-society hall could be easily added and arranged.

A chapter house would do the fraternity much good, and would give Omega a permanency that would resist the ordinary mutations of a chapter life. When one considers the influence for good by such a simple method as this, no time should be lost to establish a chapter house. Omega has an important mission to perform. She has, and will have, young men intrusted to her care who will appreciate the increased facilities of literary and social surroundings. It is believed a chapter house would help in this good work more than anything else at present.

The work of the literary societies in the University is now transferred to the secret fraternities. Every week meetings are held, and they are literary as well as social in their character. What is now being done in this way by Omega is a valuable auxiliary for educating and perfecting young men. The work accomplished has been excellent, and is fully recognized and esteemed by professors and students alike. No better testimony could be given of the worth and importance of our chapter work than that of our esteemed brother, W. Scott Mathew, '76, who says: "Among the most delightful and *profitable* associations in my life, thus far, I count those in Sigma Chi. May she lift up her standard for a thousand years."

There is abundant reason to be proud of the record of Omega. A house dedicated to her honor would give her a prestige over rival fraternities, and would increase and make more brilliant her splendid achievements. It would be a home for all Sigma Chis who return to these classical shades, or for the pilgrims of the white cross whose wanderings bring them in this direction. The Omega chapter house will soon be an assured fact. The pleasant dream of a house of our own will, it is sincerely hoped, be realized in the near future.

III—A MATTER OF POLICY.

The studied policy which Omega has maintained all through her history, in soliciting men to become her members, has been fruitful of good results. This policy has been combated by the opposition fraternities in a spirit bordering on ferocity, and with misrepresentations as malignant as they have been unjust. Omega has been accused of all manner of deceitfulness and corruption by her contemporaries in order to prejudice students against her. In all this tirade against her character, she has not so much as lifted her voice, as she could have done, to sound the demerits, shallowness and vice of her opponents. Her policy has been simply that rule which is termed golden, "Do unto others as you would have them do unto you." No one will question the wisdom of this broad and humanitarian policy, which is stamped as the best in all civilized and enlightened nations. It may seem a new idea for a fraternity to adopt, especially when the strife for men becomes fierce and desperate; but we earnestly believe it is the only true and manly way of conducting a fraternity. It can do no possible good for one to abuse the character of the men of another fraternity, or to attach a stigma of vice or corruption to one member with the view of bringing disgrace and defeat to his brotherhood. We hold it to be a truth, that a fraternity which has not enough principle, morality and intelligence to base its merits upon, without decrying its opponents and attempting to belittle them, is not the fraternity for a man to join. Competition is necessary, but honorable and fair competition is the only true method of conducting a fraternity composed of gentlemen. We are not claiming for Omega or Sigma Chi that all her members have been the truest and best men in the universe; nor do we imagine for a moment that our contemporary Greeks would claim as much for their men. It would be absurd. We possess, however, a high ideal as to what a brother in our order should be, but if that ideal is not attained, the individual, not the fraternity, is at fault. We do know that a large majority of our brothers approach very nearly to the high mark of character desired; and it is our object to make them better, and the fraternity stronger, by exhibiting the merits of our order, rather than by tearing down the character of our opponents, and thus by comparison making ourselves greater. We prefer a campaign of merits to the pernicious doctrine of sounding demerits. No fault can be laid at the door of this fraternity on that account. If the teachings and discipline of the Sigma Chi Fraternity were fully learned and heeded, no one, not the most hot-headed objector to secret societies, could find fault or say aught against it. Let our opponents say what they will, but let Omega maintain her dignified, courageous and Christian policy of good will to all men, and in the end the wise and righteous cause of Sigma Chi will prevail. Our contemporaries cannot fail to see ere long the wisdom of our course, and respect and honor us for it.

CHAPTER XX.

THE INTERCOLLEGIATE LITERARY ASSOCIATION.

THIS association was first suggested by Col. T. W. Higginson, in *Scribner's Monthly* for January, 1873. The subject was discussed by students, professors and literary men in the newspapers and magazines until February, 1874. At that time the idea crystallized into a visible form. The students at Princeton College opened a correspondence on the subject with those of Williams. This correspondence resulted in a call being issued and sent to the leading colleges of the United States. It invited each of the colleges to send three delegates to an Intercollegiate Literary Convention to be held at Hartford, Conn., February 19, 1874. The object of the convention was briefly this:

It had long been a subject of reproach that students from different institutions never met as contestants, except to display their physical powers, and it was thought that contests in scholarships, essay writing and oratory might be both pleasant and profitable. It was believed that they would increase public interest and individual devotion to literature and science; that the efficiency of our colleges would be greatly increased, and that they would give an incentive for better results, both among students and professors. If successful, they would prove a salutary and efficient antidote to boating and other sporting predilections evinced by many of the colleges, and would no doubt recall the students to their books by stimulating the powers of the mind and by firing their ambition for a higher and better culture.

Fourteen colleges responded to the call, and the association was duly organized.

The first prize contest was in 1875. The prizes and other expenses were paid by the contribution of wealthy people of New York. The management of the association was in the hands of undergraduates, and it bade fair to grow in strength and importance, and become a potent factor in the education of college men.

The Northwestern University was not represented until January, 1876, when she was admitted and sent competitors to the different departments. In April, 1875, a meeting of the students was held, and after adopting the constitution and by-laws of the Intercollegiate Literary Association, a plan was devised for the selection of representatives. It was decided to hold a preliminary oratorical contest in September; citizens of the village to be the judges; the one taking the first prize to go to New

York, and the second to Jacksonville, where the Interstate oratorical contest would be held. The orators elected were W. Scott Mathew, J. F. Stout, F. M. Taylor, T. B. Hilton, Jr., F. M. Bristol and John Krantz. On September 30 the preliminary contest was held in the Congregational Church, and all the contestants appeared except Mr. Stout. The first prize was awarded to Frank M. Bristol, and the second to W. Scott Mathew. This contest was a remarkable one, inasmuch as every oration was finely written and well delivered, but no one at that time could deliver an oration like Mr. Bristol, or put heart and soul into it as he could.

On January 4, 1876, the second oratorical contest took place in New York city. There were eleven colleges represented. Cornell, Hamilton, Princeton, Williams, Lafayette, College of the City of New York, Syracuse, St. John's, University of the City of New York, Rutgers and Northwestern University. Julian M. Elliot, of Hamilton, received the first prize in oratory. His subject was, "The Heroic Element in Modern Life." J. D. Tompkins, of Cornell, took the second prize. The subject of Mr. Bristol's oration was, "Hunger," and the reports in the papers spoke very highly of his effort. The judges were William Cullen Bryant, Whitelaw Reid and Geo. W. Curtis. On the subject for essay, "Dickens and Thackeray Compared," Cornell took first and Williams the second prize. The prize for the best essay, on "The Advantages and Disadvantages of Universal Suffrage," was divided between N. S. Spencer, of the College of New York, and Frank A. Hills, of the Northwestern University. Frank M. Harris, '75, contested for the prize in mathematics. The next day the Intercollegiate Convention was held, and John H. Hamline was chosen secretary. Mr. C. P. Wheeler represented N. W. U. at this convention.

The election of men for these contests was always spirited. The different candidates had their enthusiastic friends and admirers, and plans were generally carefully laid a long time before the day of election. The feeling between the different fraternities ran very high sometimes in the effort to elect their particular candidates. Sometimes the tricky and questionable methods of the ward politician were adopted in order to secure the majority of votes, but as a rule the contests were honest and manly. It was a great honor to go to New York and represent the University at these contests. Ours was the only Western institution belonging to the association. It was justly considered much more important than to be on the program for any of the local contests. The men going there were brought in contact with the best class of college men. Their ideas were broadened, their aspirations were stimulated, and they returned with a keener and better relish for hard, studious work. An excellent opportunity was afforded to study the methods and results of Eastern-bred men.

In the Fall of 1876 the contest for selecting delegates was perhaps the fiercest. Eight men had been elected in May, 1876, to compete for the privilege of going to New York as the orator, but only two prepared for the contest, and the decision, after all, was left to the students. It was generally conceded in the college that F. M. Taylor was entitled by his preëminent ability to represent us in mental science, and he was elected both for this department and as essayist without opposition.

The real contest was for the orator. Sigma Chi had her representative in the person of W. S. Mathew, and Beta Theta Pi had F. H. Scott. Mathew had had considerable practical experience and had made an excellent impression as an orator. Mr. Scott, his opponent, was quite young, and had appeared in public only a few times. He was naturally bright and active, and at this time was working hard. His ambitious friends were no doubt more determined than he was, and adopted methods not exactly fair or just. Sigma Chi was represented as selfish and political; rumors calculated to do her injury were set in motion, and the contest virtually was between Beta Theta Pi and the field against Sigma Chi. Anything to beat Sigma Chi. The merits of the men cut no figure in the contest. Mr. Scott was finally chosen the orator. He went to New York and delivered his oration, but he was nearly sick at the time and failed to secure the prize. The contestant in mental science was Fred. M. Taylor, and he secured the second prize. The contestants for essay prizes were Fred. M. Taylor and C. H. Morgan. Mr. Taylor took the first prize in essay, making $250 prize money secured by one man, not to mention the honor and distinction. Mr. Taylor took for his subject "The Position of Hawthorne in American Literature." The news of Taylor having taken two prizes was received with the greatest enthusiasm. It was a great day for the University, for Sigma Chi and for Taylor. When he returned a large crowd met him at the station and gave him a grand welcome. The familiar yell, " Rah, Rah, N. W. U.—OO—O, O!" was given with an energy and spirit worthy of the cause. On January 14 the Omega chapter gave Bro. Taylor an elaborate banquet, and filled him with such evidence of good will as would cheer his heart and comfort his soul as long as memory lasts.

There were no contestants in mathematics or Greek. A. W. McPherson was chosen for the contestant in Latin.

Our representative to the contest in January, 1878, was Conrad Haney. He started for New York in high glee. Having been the recipient of a new beaver hat and an extra brand of imported cigars, he had his picture taken and was sent on his way rejoicing. He had a good oration and made a favorable impression on the audience.

Miss Elizabeth R. Hunt, '77, was the essayist and was awarded the prize, but unfortunately she received only one quarter of it.

New men of recent college graduation, with little experience, had managed the association badly. They put forth large promises without any means of fulfilling them. Prizes amounting to nearly $2,000 were offered, with only $500 in the treasury; and, worse than all, no effort was made to obtain more. The prize-winners of '78 received only 25 per cent, and this was taken from the amount remaining in the treasury from the previous year. This had a very depressing effect on the whole association, and in '79 there was a decided lack of interest manifested. Our University that year was represented in the Oratorical and Latin departments. Mr. W. H. Harris, '78, was the orator, and took for his subject, "The Duty of the American Scholar in Politics." Bro. Harris' effort was unexceptionably well received. W. H. Wait, '79, contested for the prize in Latin. This was the last contest of the association. The deplorable action of the managers alienated the interest once felt toward the association by New York citizens, and the prodigal use of the fees and receipts weakened the confidence originally placed in it by the colleges. It is to be regretted that the failure of the association was brought about in this manner. The object was of supreme importance to college men, and if the association could have continued it would have exerted a marked and substantial influence, not alone on the students, but on the different institutions of learning represented in it. A plan was originated and set forth in 1879, in a pamphlet by the trustees of the association, to make the prizes consist of scholarships instead of money. It did not meet, however, with any encouragement. In speaking of the contests and of the colleges represented, they paid our University the high compliment of being "that courageous, far-off University in the Northwest, whose success in winning prizes in this association has been marked, and is to be praised."

The effect of these contests on the Northwestern University was very noticeable. It was the means of presenting it to the attention of the college world in a light it had never before received. A university which could send representatives to the contests and win prizes was considered worthy of the first rank. The success of our contestants gained considerable reputation for the University. In the brief period of our connection with the association we had taken three essay prizes, and divided the honors for mental science with Princeton, which is considered among the foremost colleges in the United States in this particular branch of learning.

STATE ORATORICAL ASSOCIATION.

Another and very commendable society to which the students at Northwestern belonged was the State College Oratorical Association. It was designed to offer liberal prizes for oratorical efforts, to be given to contestants representing the different colleges in the State of Illinois. A meeting was held at Bloomington, February 7, 1874, and Northwestern was represented by M. S. Kaufman, '74, and W. L. Martin, of the same class, as delegates. The colleges represented were Northwestern University, University of Chicago, Knox College, Monmouth College, Illinois Wesleyan University, Illinois Industrial University and Shurtleff College. Aside from organizing such an association for this state, it was the plan of the promoters of this scheme to have similar associations in Ohio, Indiana, Michigan, Iowa and Wisconsin. This was accomplished in a short time. The prizes offered were $75 for a first and $50 for the second prize, and in addition to this the winner of the first prize had the honor of representing the state at the Inter-State oratorical contests.

The first contest took place at Bloomington, Illinois, November 20, 1874; J. F. Stout, '75, was the orator from Northwestern and was the winner of the second prize. The second contest was at Jacksonville, Illinois, October 28, 1875. We were represented by W. S. Mathew as the orator. The third contest was held at Evanston, October 5, 1876; Frank M. Bristol was the orator. The fourth contest was at Monmouth, October 18, 1877; George E. Ackerman was the orator from Northwestern, and he received the second prize. This was the last contest in which Northwestern appeared. Much dissatisfaction arose from the substitution of medals for cash prizes. Alterations and changes were made in the constitution particularly objectionable to our students. It was for these reasons that Northwestern withdrew from the association in October, 1878. Since then she has made no effort to enter the association, although cash prizes were afterward restored.

CHAPTER XXI.

BUILDING A GYMNASIUM.

It is not our purpose to unduly emphasize the importance and influence of the members of Omega. It seems just and right, however, to give them the full credit, which I believe has never been denied to them, for the part they have taken in the affairs which have marked the progress of the University. It can be truly said that the men of Omega have left their individual impress upon nearly every event of any importance which has occurred during the first fourteen years of our history. There were enterprises both new and important. The men of Omega were always at the front in maintaining the oratorical contests, lecture courses, the base-ball association, the boat-club crews, in procuring specimens for the museum, and in supplying amusements and recreation for the students. Such men as Collins, Lunt, Paul, Bragdon, Hamline, Taylor, Mathew, Evans, Early, Andrews and Booth were the principal leaders in every enterprise during these eventful years. They gave a wonderful impulse to everything undertaken, and success was the reward of their efforts. The citizens of Evanston and friends of the

University are greatly indebted to these men for the many pleasant and enjoyable entertainments which they were instrumental in providing.

One of the most important and noteworthy enterprises ever undertaken by the students of Northwestern University was the construction of a gymnasium. The policy of the University was of such a close and stringent character financially as to preclude the chances of building a gymnasium for many years to come. The possibility of having such a building had been discussed in the *Tripod* at different times, but it remained for Dr. C. H. Fowler, then president of the University, to give the idea currency, which he did in many substantial ways. He seemed to possess a wonderful faculty of getting other people interested, so that they would invest their money. His success as a debt-lifter in his denomination was notorious, and it was common talk that his election to the presidency of the University was largely due to this gift, which he was expected to exercise in removing the heavy debt then resting on the institution. He could get persons to purchase and donate gifts to the University where others would fail. It was through his efforts that the class of '78 bought the huge skeleton of a whale at an expense of four or five hundred dollars, to be placed in the museum as its gift. He tried to have the class of '77 buy it, but no one but the poor "bibs" were in favor of it. He was as enthusiastic over this whale business as a small boy is over a red wagon. He carried this same enthusiasm into the building of a gymnasium. The students were as a rule poor, and could hardly expect to do more than pay their ordinary expenses, but he managed to excite their hopes by telling them that they possessed wonderful abilities, and that the possibilities of young men were unlimited, and thus he got them fully interested in this scheme. The simple use of the will, he claimed, was sufficient to accomplish all things. Oneness of aim was his doctrine in life, and he carried it, body and soul into this enterprise.

In the early part of October, 1875, a circular letter was issued by W. G. Evans and Frank M. Elliot, setting forth the project of building a gymnasium, and soliciting aid from the friends and graduates of the institution. It was decided to organize under the laws of the state and to issue shares of stock. A statement was filed with the Secretary of State October 28, 1875, and soon after a license was issued to W. G. Evans, F. M. Taylor, F. M. Bristol, A. W. McPherson, F. M. Elliot, and J. A. J. Whipple as commissioners. The name given was the Northwestern University Gymnasium Association, and its object was to establish and provide for the management of a gymnasium. The capital stock was $4,000, with shares of $10 each, and its duration was for 99 years. At the first meeting of the stockholders, November 30, the following directors were elected: George Lunt, Jas. E. Deering, W. M. Booth, F. M. Bristol, J. A. J. Whipple, E. S. Monroe and G. W. Hewett. There were 129 subscribers of stock. Fourteen hundred dollars were raised by the sale of stock, which was almost exclusively taken by the students.

Work was commenced immediately. A site was procured from the University authorities in the campus on the lake shore, and a contract was let for the construction of a building. Its dimensions were 40x80 feet, with brick basement and frame superstructure, which was to be veneered with brick. This was not done, however, until 1882. A large part of the money was in hand, and the students were full of enthusiasm over this success. John Krantz, of '76, a genial, happy soul, said when the project was started: "Gymnasium ædificandum est," and it did seem as if it had hardly been started before it was built and ready for use.

On February 1, 1876, the gymnasium was formally opened. W. S. Mathew presided. A statement of the financial condition of the association was made by F. M. Taylor. Following this the Rev. W. H. Daniels delivered a very interesting and effective speech, dedicating the building as the muscle-giving temple. There was an indebtedness of $500, which was then reduced to $200, and this latter sum was paid in a short time. Then followed a very fine exhibition of athletic sports under the leadership of Prof. Charles Duplessis.

No one did more toward completing this great undertaking than Fred M. Taylor. He put his whole soul into it, and under his vigorous leadership the students lent their hearty co-operation. His valuable services will always be appreciated, for it was through his efforts that a large part of the money was raised.

Sigma Chi did her full share in this work. If the other fraternities had done half as well, the gymnasium would have been more complete. An effort was made to have each secret society donate some apparatus. The Phi Kappa Sigma Society agreed to give a health-lift, which agreement was never kept, and Sigma Chi a bowling alley. There was no delay as far as Sigma Chi was concerned, and forthwith it was put in. It was about the first piece of apparatus ready for use, and it has helped more to stimulate an interest and keep the gymnasium running than anything else connected with it. It was built in the most workmanlike manner, with all the latest improvements. A marble slab is now inserted in the west wall, covered with glass and surrounded by a neat frame, with this inscription:

> Σ   X
>
> THESE ALLEYS WERE
> BUILT AND DONATED BY THE SIGMA
> CHI FRATERNITY.
> 1876.

The general effect of the gymnasium was good. It brought the students together as they had never been before. They had a common interest and ownership in it, and all were intent upon the success of the gymnasium. It had a very marked effect on the general health of the students, and also in the increased importance of athletic sports. Its popularity grew and continued until '78 and '79. The receipts were small, and, as it was run on an economical basis, it did not more than pay the ordinary running expenses. The original stockholders now were scattered all over the country, and their interest had ceased. The new generation of students did not or could not raise money to veneer the building to protect it, and repair the worn-out apparatus. It was necessary to do something now before all would be lost or ruined. It was finally decided to have the University take the property and maintain it as a gymnasium, as it ought to have done from the very beginning. On April 24, 1880, the board of directors appointed a committee to obtain the stock from the students and transfer it to the University trustees. This transfer was to be made upon the condition that the University should complete the building and furnish it with necessary working apparatus, assume all the liabilities of the association, and to keep and maintain forever the building and apparatus in good repair for gymnasium purposes only. This committee was composed of Geo. Lunt, '72, Geo. W. Muir and E. J. Lipps, '80. The task of getting the stock certificates tried the patience and good nature of Mr. Lunt for a long time. Through his indefatigable efforts a majority of the stock was secured, and the transfer was finally made in the spring of 1881. From the first to the last, through its success and triumph in the midst of its trials and gradual disintegration, Geo. Lunt was ever the constant friend of the gymnasium. He may not have received his reward as yet for this splendid devotion, but his name will go down in history as the chief friend of and mourner for the defunct Gymnasium Association.

Dr. Joseph Cummings was elected president in

July, 1881. One of the important things he did in 1882 was to have the gymnasium put in order. He induced the trustees to spend money and fulfill their agreement with the gymnasium stockholders for veneering the building, and thus preserve it against the ravages of time. The inside of the building was also finished. In this the good doctor and the students lent a helping hand. They did all the work of casing the inside, while the University authorities simply furnished the lumber and nails. It was a busy and interesting scene to find student and president of a great University doing the common work of carpenters. New apparatus was put in, and the gymnasium is now as complete and as well equipped as the most fastidious athletic student could desire. The gymnasium was formally inaugurated under its present management February 20, 1883, with a public entertainment, in which the students and some professional athletes participated.

CHAPTER XXII.

THE BEAR STORY.

It was in November, a few days after Thanksgiving. The ground was frozen hard and the roads were very rough; here and there were small icy places. It had rained a few days before, and then the weather turned cold and froze everything up tight. The wind, as it whistled through the trees, broke the ice that had formed on them, and everywhere it was heard cracking and falling. It was just the night for some deep villainy, although the story we are to relate contains no villain or villainy. The sky was covered with a heavy mass of clouds and portended a severe storm. The moon at long intervals seemed to burn its way through the clouded vault, spread its mellow light for a moment or two, and then disappear.

Seated in a room were three students. The stove was filled with blazing red coals, which could be seen through the isinglass. On the table was a student lamp and around it the three companions were seated. They were absorbed in their work. One was rocking back and forth reading a novel; one was busy writing, getting his report ready for the weekly paper, and the other was studying Lieber's Civil Liberty. The odor of tobacco was very perceptible, two having finished their after-supper pipes, and the other was still pulling away at his silver-mounted, deeply-colored meerschaum. Presently there was a loud rap on the side door. "Come in!" all three shouted, in a tone that might well startle a stranger. The door opened, a gust of the Nor'easter preceded the person, who walked in slowly, as if uncertain of his reception at this time of night. He was large, well proportioned and athletic; his coat was buttoned up tight, with the collar rolled up. He had on a black slouch hat, and as he stood just inside the door with his hands run into his coat pockets he was not at first recognized. "Why, hello, Billy!" Dudley shouted, as soon as he discovered his old friend; "What in the world is up to-night?" Stepping forward and taking a seat near the stove, Billy in his modest way returned the inquiry, "Boys, what are you celebrating?" Dudley, acting as spokesman, replied, that Bruiser was feeding his courage on a love story, while Mac was writing up an account of his latest struggle with Bruiser. "It was such a good joke." said Dudley. "These two chums of mine provide me with any quantity of amusement. I simply stand by and quietly nudge one or the other, and very soon they will be in the midst of a heated discussion, or will be wrestling with one another to test the superiority of strength. You see, I am the audience, and at proper intervals I do the applauding. Mac, here, was all dressed up one night with all his fine togs and was going to make a call or take his girl out to an entertainment. Bruiser, more courageous than usual, put some soot on Mac's face, and, without intending it, got some of it on his rising-sun shirt front. Quick as thought Mac had Bruiser under his arm, 'in chancery,' as Baldy would say, and was scouring his face with the blacking brush. Well, if they did not cut a pretty figure, I am a goat. I thought I would split with laughter. There were daubs of black on each of their faces, a necktie missing, and their collars just hung on behind. Then they saw the ridiculousness of it all, and although they were blowing hard after the tussle, they could not help joining in the laugh. The joke became somewhat complicated when Mac discovered that he did not have another clean shirt." Billy laughed heartily, and without further delay he proceeded to business, for there was business that night that would require nerve and good management.

"You see," commenced Billy, "that bear has not been eaten yet. The boys who had charge of him did not take him to the right place." "What bear are you talking about? I've heard nothing about this," interrupted Mac. "Well, you beat me," said Billy. "I didn't suppose there was a college scrape six hours old you did not know all about. The facts in the case are these: Last Thursday, being Thanksgiving, a Mr. Jack Piedmon invited the faculty to dinner to help him eat a bear. It seems he had a young cub which he had been fattening in anticipation of this dinner. I think it was Pixney who heard of this, and he, with several other students, went down one night to the barn where the bear was kept and put it in the cellar of the old University Hall. The next morning the bear was to have been killed and prepared for the Thanksgiving feast. But the butcher, on going to the barn on his mission of slaughter, found that bruin had disappeared. This was a very sorry predicament for Mr. Piedmon, who could do nothing now but send word to the faculty that, owing to circumstances which he could not control, the dinner would be postponed. It appears that most of the members of the faculty had received other invitations for dinner on that day; but, having this previous engagement and a keen appetite for bear, they had refused them. It was certainly a great disappointment to some of them; but, by going to hotels in the city, they managed to get good dinners. The bear is now concealed in that cellar, and we have a plan to take it over in the big woods to-night and have a barbecue. We are all going to meet in — room on Orrington avenue at ten o'clock, and then we will make the final arrangements. Now, no time is to be lost. Will you all go? You can bet on a square meal, and bear roasted on a stick over the fire is something fine. I've tried it in the mountains, and it is 'away up,' I can tell you."

It did not take long for the three to decide that they could be counted in on any little game of that kind. The time was near at hand to be at the rendezvous. At the suggestion of Billy, the boys put on their oldest clothing. "I have a big knife," said Bruiser. "Take it along," replied Billy. "I have," he continued, "a blunderbuss here to blow out bruin's brains when we get to a place where it can be done without disturbing any one. In matters of this kind I dislike to disturb any one's sleep." The blunderbuss was exhibited, and proved to be a large navy six-shooter. "Why didn't you get a gatling-gun while you were about it, instead of taking this toy affair?" said Mac. "Dudley has a double-barrel shot-gun under the bed, and any quantity of ammunition. Perhaps you would like that?" "Oh, no," said Billy, "this will do the business," and he quietly put the revolver in his hip pocket. After shaking down the coal in the stove and blowing out the light, the four friends departed. "Don't be afraid, Bruiser," said Dudley. "Keep near me. It's my opinion we ought to divide up and take different directions." So Dudley and Bruiser went in one direction, and Billy and Mac in another.

The room where the boys met was small and on the second floor. Going in, one was surprised to find so many of the students interested in the barbecue. There were half-a-dozen or more seated on the bed, some down on the floor and a number were standing. In a few moments all the invited guests were present. More or less surprise was exhibited at the make-up of the crowd. Seeing a prominent theological student on the bed, Dudley approached him and expressed his surprise at seeing him, and said: "Bibs don't eat bear meat, do they?" "You just try them once," retorted the theologue.

It was decided that Pixney and Waldrond should go out and see if the bear was all right, and if he was, then another committee should go with the wagon to a certain street corner, put the bear in the vehicle and then make for the big woods as fast as possible. Pixney and Waldrond went out and made a reconnoiter and soon returned with the amazing report that the bear had disappeared. This news struck the whole company with dismay. It certainly had not been gone long, and in order to find him the company of sixteen was divided up into eight squads, each to follow certain streets and find out where the bear had been taken. This was a new element in the case, and all went out with bated breath and not a little anxious about the result. The couriers had not been out long before they had found the bear. He was being led back to the owner's barn by four big fat men, who undoubtedly believed they were doing a generous deed, and would be invited to partake of the fatted cub when he should be nicely prepared for the privileged epicures. After seeing where the bear had been placed, the two students who had followed the rescuing quartette returned to the rendezvous to report. The next hour was spent in getting word to all the other fourteen students. When the last couple was safely behind the latched door, the crowd listened with much concern to the report of those who had witnessed the return of the bear to his manger. All conversation had to be carried on in subdued tones in order not to arouse suspicion. It was finally decided that the bear must come out of his den that night, and one o'clock was the time set for the raid. Four of the pluckiest men were selected for this duty. The rest were to be scattered and be within convenient distance in case of need.

While they were waiting in this little room, packed in so close that they could scarcely move without treading on one another's toes, a hat was passed over their heads for a contribution for cider and apples. When it had gone the rounds the amount was counted, and there were twenty-nine cents. "What do you fellers mean?" shouted Simon, whose surname was Peter. "This hain't a Methodist congregation. Twenty-nine cents wouldn't buy enough cider for 'Nosey Pixney,' and he is the smallest cider drinker in the crowd. Now, boys, shell out! Bear won't taste good anyhow unless you put in a good foundation of cider and apples." With this characteristic appeal the hat went round again. Nearly every one seemed to be "strapped," and as the hat went from one to another such expressions were made as: "Busted," "Put on my other vest when I came out to-night." "Dead broke! haven't heard from home for a month," "Call again when I'm flush." This time there were sixty-three cents Simon smiled as he rattled the pennies into his capacious pocket, and remarked, "You are a wealthy set. You may eat me if you ever catch me in such a crowd of bloated bondholders again." "Oh, no, we wouldn't, Simon," shouted a voice, "*we* prefer bear."

A delegation then went out and procured a jug

of cider, some ginger snaps and apples. There was hardly enough for a taste, and it seemed only to create an appetite for more cider and more deviltry. "Boys, we must have more cider," said one. "I have a scheme," said another. "What is it?" cried a third. "I'll tell you. Leave in just enough cider in the jug to flavor the business; fill it up with water from this pitcher, and take it back and tell Mr. H—— his cider is no good. Let him judge for himself and then demand your money back." A smile was visible on every face, and signs of approval were given to this bold move of a thirsty collegian. So the committee filled the jug and started out. The grocer thought it very strange, tasted the cider and said, "being a temperance man, I am only posted on beer and such like, but it strikes me that this cider is about as you say, 'no good;'" and without making further investigation he returned the money. The committee then went to another store and got another jug of cider, and returned to the little room feeling very jubilant over its success. "You are a brick," and simultaneously the committee received an affectionate slap on the back from a number of the boys.

They were now all laughing, telling stories and smoking, when some one looked at his watch, and in sepulchral tones shouted: "Boys, the dread hour has come. It is one o'clock." Without further delay every one quieted down and made ready for the next venture. The wind continued to blow a stiff gale, and the same cracking of the ice was heard. The moon had moved a number of degrees to the west, and its subdued light was playing back and forth between the clouds like a small child at peek-a-boo.

The four who were to get the bear started, and having given the final directions to the expressman, proceeded directly to the barn where young bruin was kept. There was no trouble in getting into the barn. The bear, however, did not like the idea of taking a walk at this time of night. He growled and snapped and rattled his chain so furiously that there was danger of his arousing his owner. He was finally pacified with some lumps of sugar, led into the alley and then taken down the street toward the lake. When they had gone several blocks they met the express wagon, and then they proceeded to give bruin a ride. There was a great deal of trouble in accomplishing this, but after numerous attempts he was finally landed in the wagon with a chain attached to his neck and tied to the seat. The wagon then started, closely followed by the chosen escort.

Everything went smoothly until they reached a certain spot on Orrington avenue, north of the Woman's College. Here they were to join the rest of the party and then proceed together to the "Big Woods," where the barbecue was to take place. When the wagon stopped, the bear, unaccustomed to riding, gave a lunge forward and then backward. He came back with such force that he broke his chain and fell out over the tail-board head over heels. This stirred Mr. Bear up so much and made him so angry, that he made for the first man he saw and would have injured him but for a timely accident. Pixney was the man, and as he started to run he slipped on some ice in the middle of the road and fell. At the same time he threw his feet into the air and this so paralyzed the bear with fear that he immediately started on a run for a tree. The time he made in running was remarkable, and the way he went up that tree was a caution. There he was, away up in its branches. The tree was just beside a dwelling-house, not ten feet away. What was to be done? The boys were in a sad plight, if after all that had been accomplished, the bear was to defeat their purpose at this stage of the game. A consultation was held; it took about two minutes to decide. That blunderbuss of Billy was to be brought into requisition. The committee went to the foot of the tree and leveling it at the bear blazed away. He did not come down, so the committee fired again, and again—five times; still bruin did not budge. The firing did just what was expected. It aroused the whole neighborhood. A window went up and out popped a head. "Who are you killing?" shouted the man in the house near the tree. "Oh, no one," said Shorty; "only some of the college boys firing some crackers, that's all." Satisfied with this answer, the man pulled his head back and shut the window.

In the meantime Billy ran to Dudley's room and said: "Give me that shot-gun, quick! That blasted bear is up a tree." Rushing into the bedroom, Bruiser was discovered undressing himself preparatory to going to bed. "For the love of Fowler, what are you doing?" asked Dudley. "Is Carney coming? I—I—I thought I'd go to bed if he was," said Bruiser, in a trembling voice. "Hades!" thundered Dudley, in a deep base voice. "The best way to get out of Carney's clutches, is to get out of this room quick." It took some time, ages it seemed, to get the cartridges loaded. Everything outside had now quieted down. Men were picketed several blocks away to give the warning if policeman Carney should be coming. Every man was ready to fly in case of an attempted chase. Presently there was a loud boom, then a rustling in the branches, and down came the bear with a heavy thud. Without seeing if he was dead or alive, he was picked up and thrown into the wagon. The whole party then literally "skipped." "Where is Bruiser?" asked Dudley. "Didn't you see him," replied Shorty, "make for the Light-house after that last shot? That was a corker. Both barrels. Sounded loud as seven claps of thunder. Enough to scare any man out of his boots. Didn't see Bruiser run? No? I never saw a man run so in all my born days. He was actually half way there inside of two minutes. He made a bee-line for that Light-house, and was going as if the devil was after him. Jingo! what a gait he struck. If I hadn't yelled at him to stop he would have been at Waukegan by this time."

The party was now wending its way to the big woods west of the village. It was several miles, and, after getting down beyond the Ridge, some of the boys thought they would take a ride, among them "Shorty." Why he was called "Shorty" I do not know, for he was the tallest man in college. It was probably for the same reason that "Bruiser," "Gee" and "Stuffer" received their names, simply because "Bruiser" was quiet and demure, and "Gee" and "Stuffer" were good eaters and well kept. A number of the boys were seated on the edge of the wagon box, and "Shorty," finding no other place convenient, sat down on the bear. They had not gone far when the bear gave a tremendous groan, probably his last death gasp. "Thunder and mud! Boys, get out of the way!" screamed Shorty, as he jumped out of the wagon and vaulted a fence, scared nearly out of his wits. "Hold him down, boys," he continued, somewhat indignant at this last exhibition of the bear, "till I get the gun and settle him." It was soon discovered, however, that the animal was perfectly safe and had breathed his last. Resuming his seat, Shorty soon dropped into his usual jolly mood. Taking hold of the bear's stubby tail he gave it a vigorous shake and addressed the bear as follows: "Oh, you plantigrade quadruped! you carnivorous beast! you Ursus Americanus, why did you climb that tree, thinking you were mightier than the large-brained disciples of Prex. Fowler? Why did you scare the life out of me, you naughty thing? We shall have to eat you, won't we, boys?" "Yes, yes," chimed a number of voices. "Do you hear that, you bob-tailed vegetarian? we *shall* eat you."

It was bitter cold. The early morning air was raw and penetrating. The first thing was to have a big fire built, as soon as the party had gone far enough into the woods. A blaze was quickly started, and in a short time the flames were sending their forked tongues into the dark space above. The process of skinning the bear was simple, and, after quartering him, some choice steaks were cut off. Then each man took a stick, sharpened it, and, thrusting it through the steak, held it up to the fire. A savory smell soon began to rise. Some thoughtful one had brought salt and pepper, and soon the boys were smacking their lips in evident relish of their roasted bear. Then a story was told, and, after a good laugh, some college songs were sung. There never was a happier crowd of college boys. It was four o'clock in the morning; but what of that? It was Saturday; no recitations, and all day before them to sleep. Every one must have a relic of this latest adventure. So the claws were cut out and distributed, and then several took pieces of the skin. While all this good time was going on, some one went to see how the horses were getting along. To his surprise they could not be found. He came back and gave the alarm. The faces of the boys suddenly, as if by magic, became long and filled with a fear that they had been watched and that the horses had been stolen. A thorough search was instituted, but no horses were found. The barbecue was ended, as far as they were concerned. It was time to go home. What a long, weary walk that was. Among the many startling events which were impressed on the memory of that night of nights, none are more vivid than the memory of that walk. It will never be forgotten. It was fully six o'clock. The light over the lake was beginning to appear. Everything was as silent as a graveyard when those sixteen barbecuers were safely in their beds.

Late that day some of the boys ventured out to hear the news. The news they were expecting was not as pleasant as they had anticipated. The owner of the bear, to say the least, was indignant. Private detectives were employed to discover who had taken the bear. The faculty, it was understood, felt extremely sensitive on the subject, and would no doubt exercise a vigorous discipline on anyone found connected with the matter. All these things came before any mention had been made of the barbecue, and just in time to put the boys on their guard. No doubt the boys were thoroughly frightened. The little trophies of the bear were buried or placed out of sight. Not a word was said between these sixteen men. They hardly recognized one another, and not until a long time had passed did they venture to speak of it.

There was a great mystery, too, about it all. Reports crept into the papers, and some remarkable explanations were set forth to explain how the bear might have escaped of his own accord. The Davis street sewer was being built at that time, and it was said that the bear had broken out of the barn, and in his perambulations had fallen into the ditch and was lost in the sewer. Another report was that the bear had been seen in the cemetery at Calvary. The bear had on a number of occasions really broken out of the barn. One evening one of Mr. Piedmon's neighbors, a large, portly man who keeps a stable, was going along the street, and up behind him came the bear. Thinking it was a dog, he spoke patronizingly to it. The bear brushed up against his legs and gave a fierce growl. Mr. Neighbor jumped and said something in a very terrified and emphatic manner.

Probably no one received as much benefit from the mystery of this bear's disappearance as the parents of children who were in the habit of running away. The simple statement that the bear would eat them up, or would catch them, was sufficient to maintain the required discipline over the children of the household.

All these things were very amusing to the barbecuers, especially as they were instrumental in having these wild rumors set in motion. They mystified the detectives, and caused them to make vain searches in other directions. An expressman was arrested and brought before a Justice, but the evidence was not enough to convict him in the matter, and he was discharged. Suffice it to say that no outsiders ever knew what became of the bear, or who took it away.

But the disappearance of that team that night was for years a mystery to those sixteen men. At this late date, however, it is partially explained. The night the owner with his friends recovered the bear, he was summoned to the door by a ring of the bell. On opening it he found no one there, but he saw a piece of paper on the steps. He picked it up and went into the house. It read as follows: "You will find your bear in the cellar of the old University building." Acting on this information, he immediately went with his friends and took the bear to his house. Now, who sent him that note? Evidently some one who thought the joke had gone far enough. There were two distinct parties in this bear escapade. One party was satisfied with simply taking the bear and keeping it until after Thanksgiving, and then returning it to the owner. This party informed the owner where the bear was kept, and it was undoubtedly this wing of the bear party that took the horses and returned them, being particular to put them in their owner's barn. Everything was returned except a horse blanket, but the expressman was paid for that. The other party wanted the fun of eating the bear, and with this in view invited a number of friends to join them. This was done with the result as already related.

This college experience is regarded by the students of N. W. U. as one of the most exciting and thrilling adventures in all the annals of the University. In later years it has been told a great many times, and many improbable incidents have been added to it. The account as here given is believed to be trustworthy. We are confident, however, that a great many interesting details of it yet remain unwritten, and we hope at some future day some one of the participants in it will do the subject full justice.

CHAPTER XXIII.

THE CONVENTIONS OF SIGMA CHI.

First Biennial Convention, June 28, 1857, at Cincinnati, O.

Second Biennial Convention, April 17-18, 1861, at Wheeling, W. Va.

Third Biennial Convention, July 6, 1864, St. Charles Hotel, Pittsburgh, Pa.

Fourth Biennial Convention, April 11, 1865, Burnet House, Cincinnati, O.

Fifth Biennial Convention, December 27, 1865, St. Charles Hotel, Pittsburgh, Pa.

Sixth Biennial Convention, December 27-28, 1866, Law Buildings, Columbian University, Washington, D. C.

Seventh Biennial Convention, December 31, 1868, and January 1, 1869, Odd Fellows Hall, Louisville, Ky.

Eighth Biennial Convention, December 28-29, 1870, Upsilon Chapter Hall, Philadelphia, Pa.; J. Frank Robinson, Omega delegate.

Ninth Biennial Convention, December 26-27, 1872, Neil House, Columbus, O.

Tenth Biennial Convention, October 21, 22, 23, 1874, Exchange Hotel, Richmond, Va.; Daniel C. Riehl, Omega delegate.

Eleventh Biennial Convention, October 11, 12, 13, 1876, Theater of the Amateur Drawing Rooms, on Seventeenth street, Philadelphia; Frank E. Knappen, Omega delegate.

Twelfth Biennial Convention, November 19, 20, 21, 1878, Knights of Pythias Hall, Indianapolis, Ind.; Edward L. Stewart, Omega delegate.

Thirteenth Biennial Convention, November 16, 17, 18, 1880, National Hotel, Washington, D. C.; R. V. DeGroff, Omega delegate.

Fourteenth Biennial Convention, November 7, 8, 9, 1882, Grand Pacific Hotel, Chicago, Ill.; George P. Merrick, Omega delegate.

Fifteenth Biennial Convention, August 27, 28, 29, 1884, Burnet House, Cincinnati, O.; Charles S. Slichter, Omega delegate.

At the third and fourth conventions there was no quorum, the former being attended exclusively by the Pennsylvania chapters and the latter only by delegates from Alpha, Xi, Rho and Lambda. There was no convention in 1859. No delegate was present from Omega at the ninth convention.

CHAPTER XXIV.

SIGMA CHI SENTIMENTS.

"YE brethren of the old Hellenic tie,
The fair fraternity of Sigma Chi;
What though your temple, gentle sons of peace,
Rears not its altars 'mid the groves of Greece."

      W. W. FOSDICK,
        Lambda, 1861.

From an address delivered before the Thirteenth Biennial Convention of the Sigma Chi Fraternity at Washington, D. C., November 18, 1880.

You are gathered here from all parts of the country—each one identified with some institution of learning in the land,—the prejudices of no section, however bitter, affect the catholic spirit of your order. It blooms with as much fragrance amid the cold winds of the North as it does under the warm rays of a Southern sun.' But stronger even than this tie is the bond that unites you as co-laborers in the same harvest field. You are gathering, it is true, in different parts of the field, but in the same field you are gathering the same harvest, and binding and storing the full, rich sheaves of learning and knowledge.

You are bound together by the same sympathies of a common service, and soon, very soon, when the fullness of your preparation is come, and the master dismisses you with your Alma Mater's blessing, amid the tumult and the dazzle of the busy world, when the stern realities of life confront you, when the curtain is withdrawn and you are introduced on the great stage of the every-day, practical working world, with throbbing pulse, with apprehensions and misgivings, it may be, yet inspired with the buoyancy and confidence of youthful enthusiasm, each one will be found asking himself the same pregnant question: "What part am I to play in the drama of life on this great stage?"

LINDEN KENT,
Psi.

To the world outside societies like ours mean but little; but to us who realize their benefits, who have enjoyed their pleasures, who associate them with everything that was agreeable in our college life, and who in them have found friendships that will last with life, they mean a great deal. We are Greeks, and we know how to appreciate them.

I congratulate you upon the high standing of your society, and upon the bright prospect before it in the future. I feel the highest pleasure and satisfaction in being one of its founders; and I

regard every member of it with sentiments of the warmest and most sincere friendship; and I trust the chain which unites us may never be broken. HON. I. M. JORDAN,
Old Alpha, 1857.

From an address delivered before the Fourteenth Biennial Convention, at Chicago, Nov. 9, 1882.

Many years have placed themselves between my acquaintance with the active life of the fraternity and the present time—many years of busy activities and the realities of life, until its formalities and its ritual had almost disappeared from my mind. But this occasion recalls many a pleasant memory of my college days, and what I regard as the most pleasant of my recollections, when with ceaseless watch and toil we sought to found the structure of our future lives, when we enlivened with kindly mirth and fraternal communication the labors of our college days. These pleasing memories, as I meet you again in conclave here to-night, come back to me on wings of thought.

*   *   *   *   *   *

Let the principles of this fraternity be the cultivation of the social side of man's nature as well as his intellect, to teach him to measure himself and his fellow-men, so that by contact with those above him he may inquire into the most secret springs which move human action. Thus may he develop his character and make his education truly and properly complete. Let it be known that it is a principle of this organization to cultivate the social graces, to stamp out the social vices. Let it be understood that, while we are looking forward to the training of the mental powers, while the cultivation of the intellect is a main purpose of Sigma Chi, the higher qualities of general culture and polish are of equal importance. One may have passed with honor through college halls, and yet be poorly equipped for the battle of life. The world cares little for standing in classes. Your success will be measured by your ability to estimate and gauge humanity; and you can only be skillful in your judgment of men by close communication and affiliation with men. Let these emblems of our fraternity, therefore, stand for these principles of culture and education, and hostility to us as an organization will cease. . . . Let the emblem of the White Cross of Sigma Chi be an emblem of our purity and devotion to the principles of honor and manhood, of unwavering devotion to humanity. Let it be your emblem, not only in college, but as you go out into the world let it be a decoration indicating that you have been tried in your early manhood by your fellow-men, and found true in your friendships and devotion to principle. In after life you will find many occasions in which this training of the fraternity may be of use to you.

GOVERNOR JOHN M. HAMILTON,
Alpha, 1868.

The present tendency of the Greek world is toward concentration and centralization. Your Greek Press Association, your Pan-Hellenic councils, and the tone and spirit of fraternity journalism,—all declare, in language unmistakable, that the day of the loose confederation of heterogeneous chapters has passed away forever. The fraternity of the future is to be a federation of harmonious parts, each working for the interest of the whole. The progress which is visible in nearly every phase of fraternity life and work is progress upon lines which converge toward each other and meet in a universal progress toward centralization. The day is coming when, more than ever before, the several chapters of every Greek order will stand or fall upon the merits of the entire fraternity.

WALTER L. FISHER,
Chi, 1883.

Of all the secret societies I have known, none offer more attractions or advantages than ours to young men. Its aims and purposes are lofty and honorable in all particulars. It ought to succeed; it has succeeded and it will succeed. If friendship among young men at college is of any value, if the companionship of the good and the gifted should be cultivated, if sympathy and assistance in the performance of duty are of any advantage, then, indeed, our society was not founded in vain, and it will grow and prosper, and the name of Sigma Chi will be everywhere a passport of honor and respectability.

Hon. Isaac M. Jordan,
Old Alpha, 1857.

No person should be admitted to membership who cannot promote the general welfare of the fraternity by bringing with him a clean character, lofty aims, and his due share of mental and moral stamina. And last, but not least, he should be a man who possesses the sterling quality of good fellowship—who can be a true companion to his associates, who can at all times rise out of self and think and feel for others. Made up of such material, a fraternity cannot be otherwise than a constant source of benefit and pleasure to those who form it. Edwin L. Shuman,

Omega, 1887.

I have been requested to say something touching the influence of Greek Letter Societies upon students and student life. Little need be said; every sensible, practical man knows that social and literary clubs are as necessary to the student as tea parties to old maids, or whist clubs to old bachelors. "Man cannot live by bread alone," and no more can the live American student exist on a diet of Greek and Latin roots, spiced with diabolical mathematical conundrums and washed down with solemn moral homilies. In these societies literary exercises go hand in hand with social recreation. The influence of these associations cannot be other than healthful and beneficial. The friendship formed in these fraternities, when men's hearts are pure and unselfish, endures through life, and the hours passed in these halls are the most fondly cherished memories of our college days. As long as the American student exists these fraternities will flourish, and those who make war upon them should remember that persecution is a wonderful stimulant to rapid growth.

     COL. BEN. P. RUNKLE, U. S. A.,
       Old Alpha, 1857.

I regard secret societies, such as ours, the lawful and natural outgrowth of college life. Such societies have existed in most of our American colleges from a very early day, and they will continue to exist as long as the institutions where they are situated. They do not exist by mere sufferance, but by right. They can be defended as well in the forum of law as of justice.

Hon. Isaac M. Jordan,
Old Alpha, 1857.

Then as Now—Gleanings from Some Old Letters.

"We received a letter yesterday from Nashville. There is a branch of the $\Delta K E$ there and the petitioners wish to start an opposition. We have given them the necessary instructions, so our cause prospers."

"We have adopted A as the name of our chapter, and as you do not wish to be called B, yours will be Γ."—J. Parks Caldwell, A, to Charles Reynolds, of O. W. U., May 3, 1856.

"Hon. G. A. Parker accepts membership and writes us a very fine letter. He expects to be with us next summer, and says it will give him great pleasure to meet us. Rev. Mr. Richardson, of Hamilton, has received the vote of this chapter for honorary membership, with the expectation that he will act as chaplain at our convention."

"Our chapter is in a most flourishing condition. We have twelve members: five seniors, three juniors, one sophomore and three freshmen. The $\Delta K E$'s, the objects of our eternal hostility, have dwindled down to one wretched, solitary member. The Φ Δ Θ's number four seniors and one freshmen. The Δ Κ Φ's have internal commotions and "cuss" each other like the inhabitants of Pandemonium, notwithstanding their members in the faculty and their consequent high grades. The Β Θ Π's are very friendly and have some splendid fellows. The Β Φ's are too contemptible to mention. Among all these the cross is honored. 'Esto perpetui.'

"We expect to hold our convention on the 18th and 19th of June next. What can your chapter do for us financially in the coming convention? Our fellows are all well known here—Ben tells me to say especially to creditors—and we expect our lions to come from our other chapters. We expect to give $125 at least."—T. C. Bell, Α, to Charles Reynolds, Γ, January 26, 1857.

"We also have the gratifying news of an organization at the University of North Carolina, which will petition shortly."—Frank H. Scobey, Α, to B. F. Barger, Γ, February 14, 1858.

"The place selected could not have been more happily chosen. In the soil of the old Dominion let the true-souled sons of the North and South meet together. Let us lay aside party spirit and sectional prejudice, and, taking our Southern brethren by the hand with the magic grip, let us use our influence to bring them back to the glorious old Union, to bring them again under the shadows of that time-honored banner that has been our common pride and protection. Let the Stars and Stripes float over the assembled convention, and the old national airs stir up the patriotic souls of Sigmas. By the soul of Washington, gentlemen, I will be with you. This is a slender thread, but all the Abolitionists and Disunionists out of hell cannot sever it."—Letter of March 22, 1861, of Benj. F. Runkle to Frank Baker, I', accepting invitation to be present at the Wheeling Convention.

LOUISVILLE, February 18, 1861.

My Dear Sirs,—I desire to express my thanks for the honor your society has conferred by creating me an honorary member, and also by appointing me its poet for the convention at Wheeling.

But I shall be obliged to decline the appointment of poet, for my duties at home, editorial and otherwise, and my health will make it impossible for me to accept the honor and fulfill its office.

With many assurances of my kindest regard,
   I remain very truly,
     GEO. D. PRENTICE.

To MESSRS. F. J. FITZWILLIAM, JAS. W. NEWMAN.

WASHINGTON, D. C., April 5, 1861.

My Dear Sir,—You must forgive me for the apparent sentimentality of writing with my heart's blood. If you were a young lady whose name begins with an anonymous letter of the alphabet, it would doubtless be very appropriate. But the red ink happened to be nearer my pen. You may expect me to be present at the Wheeling occasion. If I am not there you may consider it providential—in whatever sense you please. I shall make my best endeavor, however. Please let me know where I may find you on arriving at Wheeling. I shall probably get there on the afternoon of the 17th.

Very truly your friend,
JOHN J. PIATT.

To JAMES W. NEWMAN, ESQ.

"Seven men again! We began with seven—your petition with seven—our brothers of Nashville sent the same number of names attached to their petition, and here we have the magic number again presented to us."—Frank H. Scobey *A*, to M. B. Clayson, *Γ*, in a letter of May 20, 1857, conveying the petition from the University of Mississippi.

"Below I give you a copy of the petition received from the students of Erskine College, South Carolina. Some of the petitioners are personally known to our members, who highly recommend them. The college is one of very good standing, having about 200 students."—Thos. E. Tucker, *H*, to Jas. W. Newman, *I*, January 13, 1859.

"Our prospects are now quite flattering, indeed. We are twenty-nine in number."—W. J. Dennis, *II*, to Jas. W. Newman *I*, May 7, 1860.

"I will explain why (in my opinion) you think there is some lingering distrust in the minds of some of our Southern brethren. When this college was first opened after the war, we who came here were all strangers to each other, and knew nothing of ΣX, $\Delta K E$, $\Delta \Psi$, $\Sigma A E$. There were no Sigma Chis here then. Brother H. C. Myers and I were acquainted with some old Sigma Chis and wrote to them for a constitution. They exerted themselves and procured a copy of the constitution of the chapter, formerly at Lagrange, Tennessee, before the war, which they sent us. We tried to get them to come and reorganize us, but they could not. We set to work, however, and reorganized the chapter with no other aid than the constitution. This did not help us much. It was some time before we were able to keep our heads clear of the water, but Providence crowned our efforts with success, and it will not be long before we are first in this college. You see we were unacquainted with the minutiæ of writing letters to the different chapters. The constitution said we should have all our correspondence stamped with the secret motto. Well, here was another trouble to us. We had no stamp, and the letters of the motto did not tally with those of the alphabet, but we finally made it out. We did not express ourselves as freely in our first letter as we desired, because we were apprehensive that we would not be welcomed into the bonds of the fraternity, but I am now happy to state that all such apprehensions are allayed by the letters received from our sister chapters of the North."—Letter of June 2, 1866, from Wallace Wood, *H*, to Harry Ufford, *P*.

Memento Mori.

The swift years roll on, my brothers;
   Let us clasp each other's hand;
Let us do our work together,
   While we still are all one band.

Some beside the way have fallen;
   Sadly think we of the dead;
But the stronger let us labor
   Each with heart and hand and head.

Let the thought of them inspire us
   To do what they would have done,
That no task may be unfinished
   At the setting of our sun.

A S. E.

CHAPTER XXV.

NECROLOGY.

I.

EVARTS GREENE BOUTELL.

DIED MAY 21, 1870.

Aged 15 years, 7 months and 5 days.

The first sorrow that comes to a united household seems always the hardest to bear; the first death the greatest calamity. Omega had been in existence scarcely a year when the grim Angel of Death suddenly appeared and took from her one of the most promising and devoted of her members. For the first time in her history death invaded her circle of chosen friends. The blow, which fell with unexpected violence, was not only severely impressed upon her members, but was received with evidences of profound grief throughout the whole community. It is of slight importance whether a child or a patriarch dies, but that a life should be suddenly extinguished is a matter that should fill us with deep meditation and receive our careful consideration.

The deaths which have come to our chapter have fallen on young men; those who were just beginning to give evidences of the greatness that was in them. The aspiring minds and noble souls of these men were suddenly cut off from the great life-current of earth, and their careers ceased. We do not think of them as dead, but as living, enshrouded by the spirit of love and peace. We prefer to think of them as the Northmen do of their dead friends. Their "image of death is finer than that of other climes; no skeleton, but a gigantic figure that envelops men with the massive folds of its dark garment." The dark robe is drawn around our departed brothers and they are lost to our view.

Evarts Greene Boutell was born at Westborough, Worcester county, Massachusetts, October 16, 1854. His father, Mr. Lewis H. Boutell, is one of the recognized leaders of the Chicago bar. Evarts had two brothers and one sister. Henry S. Boutell was younger, but was his constant companion up to the time of his death. Probably no two brothers were ever more devoted to one another than Evarts and Harry. They pursued their work together, and in their joy and play their mirth was mingled with a deep brotherly love. They enjoyed the superior advantages of a correct and intellectual environment. Their parents possessed strong intellectual faculties and their home was one of progressive thought and refinement. The early boyhood of Evarts was passed in Massachusetts, where he was under the influence of an atmosphere charged with the ripest scholarship. If he had been a dull boy he would have felt the influence for good by these surroundings. But he inherited strong intellectual traits. He had a clear head and could grasp an idea and see it in all its varied shades of meaning. It seemed the simplest thing in the world for him to learn. No effort was required apparently for him to master a subject or a study. For one so young this brilliancy of intellectual grasp was remarkable. In 1865 Major Boutell sent his family to Evanston, where he soon followed after his discharge from the army. In 1867 Evarts entered the Preparatory department of Northwestern University. He commenced the classical course, but his aptitude for scientific researches led him to give as much attention to science as to the classics. This combination so largely developed in his mind was extraordinary. In the classics he was at the head of his class, and no one excelled him in the study of the sciences. He had a great love for nature. He thoroughly explored all this part of the country, and in all his excursions his brother Harry was with him. In the fields or in the laboratory they were together. They made extensive collections, especially of insects. They were enthusiastic and worked with scientific accuracy, and all their work was done in good taste. They did a great deal for the museum of the University. The whole collection of insects was arranged and labeled by them, and they added to it from their own a large number of species, especially of Lepidoptera. The work still remains much as they left it. One of the professors, in speaking of Evarts, says: "He was naturally a leader; he had great pleasure in all intellectual as well as physical activities, and he was enthusiastic in the attainment of his ends. Still he was quiet and kindly. To all appearances the sad accident which terminated his life blotted out a brilliant future."

It was soon after Omega was established that Evarts Boutell was initiated into the Sigma Chi Fraternity. He was greatly esteemed and loved by all the members. The bond was reciprocal. Evarts was as enthusiastic over Sigma Chi, as he was over everything else that he loved and admired. He was quite intimate with Brother Fenemore E. Hancock, who was the next one to leave the chapter by death, and join his brother Sigma Chi in eternity. In the resolutions adopted by the Philomathean Society, commemorating the death of Brother Boutell, the following appears to have been written by Brother Hancock: "That we cherish his worthy example, and, realizing more fully the uncertainties of life, we dedicate ourselves anew to the life-work before us, and, bowing in submission to Heaven's will, we strive to emulate his examples."

The story of Brother Boutell's death is brief and sad. While on one of those pleasure excursions which he frequently made, in company with his brother Harry and a friend by the name of Arnold, he went hunting south of the village near Calvary. In the course of their walk they came to the lake, and securing a boat went out for a short ride. When they returned and were landing, as their gun was being lifted from the boat, it was discharged, and the whole shot entered Evarts' mouth and lodged in his brain, causing instant death. Expressions of praise for the departed and of sympathy for the family were universal. This tragic ending of one so gifted by nature and so highly esteemed and loved by all who knew him, was peculiarly sad and caused a pang in many hearts. His funeral took place May 23, 1870. Rev. E. N. Packard made the funeral address, from which a few passages are selected. "The life so suddenly snapped off here, beginning only fifteen years ago last October, leaves but a short simple record for *words*, deep as that record may be in our hearts. Yet few longer lives can sum up better. Young as Evarts was, he had acquired a character, marked clearly and well, and established on firm foundations. He had gained in this community, as you will all bear me witness, what Solomon calls better than great riches—a good name. Lads are hardly aware how early the eye of the public is upon them, forecasting their future. The beginnings of true influence and success are laid in childhood. . . . No less marked were Evarts' mental traits. His mind was active, growing, truth-loving. During the past few months it seemed to develop rapidly and healthily. . . . It was his custom to commit to memory the lines of Homer which entered into the daily lessons. . . . With the genial atmosphere of home, with such healthy tastes, what rare fruits might have been expected! . . . Time, temptation, the chances and changes of life, cannot affect him. He is 'fixed in an eternal state.' He will always be the same boy to you. And where your treasure is, there will your heart be also. God takes these human ties to bind us to another world and to himself. . . . How strange a thing is life! But yesterday, and the tie that unites you and your pastor was formed. But yesterday, and the first baptism which I ever administered was of a child of this house, and now the first funeral in which I take part is in the same family. The Angels of Life and of Death have stopped at that one door so close to each other, and laid the amaranth and the asphodel side by side there."

SIGMA CHI HALL, May 25, 1870.

At a meeting of the Omega chapter, the following resolutions were adopted:

Resolved, That in the death of Evarts G. Boutell we have lost a brother whose literary talent, whose personal worth and character, whose warm, genial nature, whose many virtues and high sense of honor, have not only secured him a lasting reputation among the members of our order, but have endeared him to all who ever enjoyed his society or friendship.

Resolved, That the untimely death of Bro. Boutell has deprived our fraternity of one of its most devoted and ardent members; while his relatives and friends must mourn one who not only reflects honor upon them, but also bade fair to take high rank in the social, scientific and literary circles of life.

Resolved, That, as a mark of respect due to his memory, we will wear the usual badge of mourning of the order for the usual time.

Resolved, That a copy of these resolutions be forwarded to the *Evanstonian* for publication; also that a copy be communicated to the relatives of the diseased, with the expression to them of our warmest sympathy and condolence in their great bereavement.

A. D. LANGWORTHY,
M. C. BRAGDON,
LORIN C. COLLINS,
Committee.

The following letter, recently written to the editor by Professor Robert Baird, illustrates the mental characteristics and worth of Bro. Boutell:

"I remember Evarts," says Professor Baird, "as one of those boys who are an inspiration to an instructor, and whose tragic death, coming as it did in the early years of my teaching, impressed me as nothing since has impressed me. Traditions of his wonderful ability lived long in the memory of his class ('74); but while I recognize this, what seemed most remarkable to me was the ease with which he did his work. Most students who show great ability manifest also a wearing intensity, a nervous strain that makes known what their achievements cost. But Evarts always seemed perfectly at his ease, under no strain, making no effort, performing the severest tasks as if he were going through a mere business formula which he was repeating for the hundredth time. In his conduct he seemed to do what he wanted to do and yet what was just right. I cannot recall that I ever had occasion to reprove or correct him, though I never knew him, so far as I could see, to make any effort to behave himself. I remember my own surprise at a display of his ability out of the lines in which we usually saw them. It was at the end of the term, and the class were writing essays on the work we had been reading (it was the Anabasis). Some of the students had arranged their essays in the form of a debate. Evarts was pitted against one nearly twice as old as himself, and in addition had the hard side of the question. I well remember the surprise of the class when he arose to read his reply to the strong plea made by the one just before him. The way in which he massed and marshaled his arguments made us see in him what we had never seen before. Everybody was astonished, and though not given to applauding, the class could hardly be restrained when he finished his argument.

It was strange but appropriate, after the terrible accident, to find on the blackboard in his well-known hand, and with his proverbial correctness, the last sentence he translated into Greek: "Let us for the present desist from the chase."

The mortal remains of Bro. Boutell were placed in the Rose Hill Cemetery.

II.

FENNIMORE ENZ. HANCOCK.

DIED FEBRUARY 16, 1872.

Aged 18 years and 9 months.

"No line which, dying, he could wish to blot."

Brother Hancock was born in Plattville, Grant county, Wis., May 3, 1853. He was the second son of John T. and Bertha E. Hancock. When quite young he went with his parents to Dubuque. The foundation of his eduction was laid in the schools of that city, where he was regarded as a boy of rare mental endowments. At the age of fourteen he attended the Agricultural College at Ames, Iowa, and remained one year. He then returned to his home, and, in a short time, came to Northwestern and entered the class of '72. He continued his studies for two years, leaving college January 1, 1871, to engage in the grocery business at Dubuque with his father.

Bro. Hancock had not been at Northwestern very long before he was recognized by the members of Omega as being a young man of unusual promise, and one who would reflect great honor on the fraternity as a member. He was initiated in 1869, and during all the time he was at college he was a devoted and enthusiastic Sigma Chi.

One of the last pictures he ever had taken was while at Northwestern, and on the lapel of his coat can be seen the badge of his fraternity.

His brother John had left college the year before and had established himself in business. It was the fond desire of his father that he and John should take up the business which he had established and in which he had been so successful, and carry it forward on its prosperous career. These fond hopes of a devoted father were dashed by the untimely death of his two sons.

In the early part of the winter of 1872 Fennimore took an extended trip through many of the southern and eastern cities with a view of broadening the field of his information and benefiting his health. The change from the cold temperature of Iowa to the damp tropical climate of Mississippi and the South was too sudden and severe for his delicate constitution, and instead of deriving benefit from this trip, he suffered physically a positive injury from it. The germs of disease were planted in his system, and upon his return home after a month or more traveling, a feeling of enervation came upon him. This continued for three weeks, when the insidious disease demonstrated its power and commenced its work of destruction. It took the form of typhoid fever, and this was accompanied and intensified by congestion of the lungs. He continued to grow weaker and weaker, and finally at the last became unconscious. On Thursday afternoon, February 16, 1872, he died. Those who stood around the couch when this young life closed saw how quietly the earthly tabernacle was left tenantless and how peacefully he slipped away without a struggle or pain. Rev. E. K. Young spoke the words of comfort to the sorrowful family and friends, and among other things gave utterance to these thoughts: "There will be something that will temper the bitterness of your sorrow, and assuage the intensity of your grief, in the thought that you can look with satisfaction and pride upon his life record. He was manly, affectionate, and courteous. Those who knew him intimately bear united testimony to this. He was ever mindful of the amenities of social life, careful of the feelings and rights of others, and thoughtful ever of the comfort and happiness of his friends."

Of Bro. Hancock the Dubuque *Daily Telegraph* gave this testimonial:

"Fennimore was a young man of superior mental ability. He possessed a clear, searching, discriminating mind, one that was evenly balanced. The education which he received served only to add additional lustre to an intellect made bright by nature. It was one of the beauties, yea virtues, of his character that no human being was ever caused pain by anything he uttered. Singularly upright in his deportment, affable in his manners, and agreeably entertaining in his conversation, he endeared himself to all those with whom he became acquainted. He loved those pleasures the province of which it is to elevate the moral and intellectual qualities, and was ever among the foremost in literary enterprises. Nurtured in a comfortable home, and surrounded by all those influences which develop the finer and nobler qualities of human nature, his life and character were reflexes of the truest type of manhood."

III.

ROBERT MARSHALL HUMPHREY.

DIED AUGUST 3, 1875.

Aged 24 years, 11 months and 3 days.

Robert Marshall Humphrey was born August 31, 1850, at Marietta, Fulton county, Illinois. His father was one of the early settlers in that county, and was engaged in farming. Robert belonged to a large family. He had eight sisters and three brothers. His father died when he was five years and his mother died when he was sixteen years old. Robert was a brave, energetic, persevering industrious boy, performing any duties assigned him on the farm in a manner unusual for one of his age. He was always one of the first in his classes in school, and at the age of twelve years he could spell every word in "Webster's Spelling Book," and spell and define every word given with definition in "McGuffey's Fourth Reader." He seemed to excel in all he attempted to learn. He was particularly fond of history, and knew the "History of the Revolutionary War" almost by heart. At the age of eighteen he left the farm and attended the Normal School at Macomb, Illinois. In September, 1869, he entered Hedding College, at Abington, Illinois, and, taking the three years' course of study, graduated in 1872. It was then his good fortune to be elected principal of the public schools at Avon, Illinois. He remained there one year. The desire for knowledge was burning within him and he determined upon taking a regular collegiate course at the Northwestern University. He entered the freshman class of 1877, and, as he was in advance of the class in some of the required work, he took at first selected studies. It was by close application that he was able to enter the Latin scientific course at the beginning of the sophomore year.

When Robert came to Evanston he had few acquaintances. His first friend was Mr. W. A. Hamilton, who became his room-mate, and with whom he shared the common vicissitudes of a college life.. But his genial and sincere qualities soon won him many friends and admirers. At the election of officers for the sophomore year, he was chosen president, an office which he filled with satisfaction to the class and with honor to himself until the time of his death.

There are not many of our old college friends whom we delight to call to memory more than "Bob" Humphrey. He was always the same studious, kind, gentle "Bob." He was never so busy that he could not lend one ready assistance over a knotty problem, or so preoccupied that he could not join in a hearty laugh over a college joke. He possessed all the traits of a gentleman, and no one who knew him could fail to respect and admire him. In February, 1875, he was initiated into the Sigma Chi Fraternity. His love for the fraternity was cordial and sincere, and he was ever ready to promote its interests and increase its strength. He was one of those constant members who allowed nothing save sickness to keep him from its meetings. The duties assigned to him were always willingly performed, and if he said he would do a thing one could be sure of its accomplishment if it were within the bounds of reason and possibility.

During the summer vacation of 1875, while visiting relations near Bushnell, Ill., he fell ill with brain fever. The disease had taken a firm hold, and after a severe sickness the spirit of him whom we cherished as a friend and a brother left us to join the silent majority. His death occurred August 3, 1875. At the regular meeting of the chapter, held on October 12, 1875, the following was adopted:

"For the first time in three years we are called to mourn the loss of a valued member of our chapter. Robert Marshall Humphrey possessed qualities that endeared him to us, and in his death the Sigma Chi Fraternity has been deprived of one who at all times and places was wholly devoted to its best interests. We desire in this brief token of respect to place on record our sense of his worth as a gentleman, a scholar and a christian. Although his life on earth was short, we feel thankful that we have had the privilege of enjoying his intimacy, and we shall ever cherish his memory. In testimony of this we will wear the badge of mourning for the usual time. To his bereaved family and friends we tender our sympathy in this our common loss."

C. R. PAUL,
A D. EARLY,
C. P. WHEELER,
Committee.

The historian of his class for the year 1876 paid him this well-deserved tribute: "Death, the infallible ruler over mortal life, visited our class and took from its midst one of its truest and most faithful members. Robert M. Humphrey entered the class in the freshman year. He followed the selected course of studies until he was able to enter the Latin scientific course a year later. He was our class president, and in this capacity he officiated up to the time of his death. Ever faithful to his studies, courteous and social, he won the esteem and friendship of all who came in contact with his genial disposition. He possessed that characteristic which is termed magnetism, and he had such a cast of mind as predicted a truly great man. Cut down in the prime of life, when his faculties were just beginning to show forth their splendor, when in a few short years he would step out into the world to do good deeds to his fellow men, one cannot refrain from inquiring why this mystery? Why this apparent sacrifice of life? We cannot explain why this should be, but we can in all humility bow to the divine will, believing that His ways are better than ours. Robert's association with us has been beneficial in many directions. Let us be thankful for these benefits, and let us emulate so far as in us lies his good example. Let us cherish his memory and commemorate his sad death with a tribute of devout respect."

In the cemetery at Marietta, Illinois, a plain

monument marks the place where Robert M. Humphrey is buried. Beside him lie the mortal remains of his parents, one brother and one sister.

IV.

HARRY PUTNEY BROWN.

DIED DECEMBER 8, 1881.

Aged 22 years, 8 months and 12 days.

Harry Putney Brown was born in Genoa, Illinois, March 26, 1859, and passed his boyhood at his father's home adjoining the village of Genoa. After an elementary training in his native village, he attended the Kane County Academy at Elgin, Illinois, until the fall of 1878, when he came to Evanston and entered the preparatory department of the Northwestern University. After a year's preparation he entered the freshman class of the University with the class of '83. His aptitude for mathematics determined his plan of study, and he decided upon the scientific course. During his freshman and sophomore years he showed great ability in scientific subjects, particularly in mathematics and chemistry. During the winter term of his sophomore year, his health not being good, he returned to his home, but again resumed his college work at the opening of the spring term. But his health did not improve, and on April 29 he left college and Evanston, and, as it proved, never to return. During the following summer he grew very much worse, and, though he struggled hard to regain his health, and was never discouraged, the insidious disease slowly but surely took possession of his weakened frame, and he died, after an illness of seven months, December 9, 1881..

Bro. Brown was an enthusiastic member of Omega chapter and thoroughly devoted to the fraternity he so dearly loved. His efforts in behalf of the chapter are kindly remembered by those who sat with him around the mystic circle, and they never will forget the cheerful face, kind looks and ever-active interest in all fraternity work so characteristic of Bro. Harry Brown.

* * *

V.

FREDERICK WILLIAM RANDOLPH.

DIED MARCH 11, 1882.

Aged 22 years, 6 months and 2 days.

Frederick William Randolph was born in the city of Chicago, September 7, 1859, and died at Lake Benton, in south-western Minnesota, March 11, 1882.

The subject of this sketch began his educational course in the public schools of Evanston, and continued his studies in the Northwestern University, where he entered with the class of '81. He subsequently passed two years at the Pennsylvania Military Academy, at Chester, in the hope of securing the increased physical development which he greatly needed. Returning in the autumn of 1879, to rejoin his class at the University, and at the same time enter its Law department, he became associated, in the following spring, with the Sigma Chi Fraternity, and remained an active member till his death. The college rules forbidding simultaneous membership in two departments prevented his taking a degree at the University, though his classmates recognized his merit as a student by awarding him their class-prophecy. From the law school he graduated with credit, taking one of the prize orations.

At a very early age he had developed a decided preference for the legal profession, for the successful prosecution of which he seemed peculiarly endowed by nature. Impatient of delay in entering upon his anticipated life work, and having a strong desire that his future professional career should rest upon foundations constructed by his own unaided efforts, he preferred to inaugurate that career single-handed and among strangers. Leaving his home at South Evanston to take up his residence and begin the practice of law at Lake Benton, Minnesota, he was, by the laws of that state, required to pass an examination before its Supreme Court, which the presiding judge pronounced the most satisfactory he had ever known. The people of Lake Benton shortly appointed him village attorney, and the ordinances which govern that now thriving city are his work.

On the evening of March 10, he retired as usual to his sleeping room adjoining and connecting with his business office. Failing to appear at both the morning and the mid-day meals of the 11th, search was instituted at his rooms, where he was found lying as in a peaceful slumber, but with the last evidence of life extinct. The cause was but too apparent. On retiring to his room he had filled the magazine of his office coal-stove; neglecting properly to close it, however, the escaping coal-gas had silently performed its deadly work, and, all unconscious and without a struggle, he had breathed his life away.

Fred Randolph might have succeeded admirably as a caricaturist, for he had rare humor with a delicate artistic sense. He possessed the kind of talent that made Nast so famous, and from him his work once received a warm commendation. But he chose to concentrate all effort in one channel. He used to quote sometimes from Earl Granville, especially that grand old sentence beginning, "Man doth not yield himself unto the angels, nor even unto death, utterly, save through the weakness of his own feeble will." It was the expression of his own earnestness and intense belief in the reality of life. Hence, though he had that rare ability which promised success in almost any direction, he worked with fixity of purpose.

Fred Randolph was a student, of course, when we boys of Sigma Chi first knew him. He came among us at a time when strong character and individuality leave their most ready impress; so we shall like him best as we knew him in those college days, when we admired his marked ability as a student and his keen humor was a power throughout the school. Neither is such a memory unjust, for the guild of student life has much in common with the world outside, and while it may not be appropriate to speculate upon the success he might have won, we may truly say that, as he had qualities of leadership, so we believed him fated for noble things.

On the sunny slope at the north end of Rose Hill, a stone bears the simple story of his twenty-two years. It seems but the record of a life begun; and yet, to those who knew and loved him well the memory has more of tenderness because the sketch, wherein the cardinal lines were so strong and true, was never finished.

* * *

VI.

JOHN S. HANCOCK.

Died January 20, 1883.

Aged 32 years, 8 months and 23 days.

John S. Hancock was born April 27, 1850, at Platteville, Grant county, Wis. His mother was of Swiss descent. His father, John T. Hancock, was an American, and was at the head of the large wholesale grocery firm of John T. Hancock & Son, at Dubuque, Iowa, which was established in 1856. When a boy, John attended the public schools of that city, and later the high school. In 1866 he went to Delaware, Ohio, and became a student in the Ohio Wesleyan University. He was in the classical course and remained there three years. In the spring of 1869 he came to Evanston, and entered the University in the class of '72. Bro. Collins, who had also been at Delaware and had come to Northwestern, was undoubtedly instrumental in bringing Bro. Hancock here. He was taken into the Omega chapter in July, 1869. His interest in Sigma Chi was always cordial and sincere, and his experiences in the fraternity were among the pleasantest in his college life. He did not remain here very long. On January 6, 1870, he was married to Miss Dora A. Stark, and in 1871 he entered the grocery business with his father. His connection with this business was maintained up to the time of his death.

Bro. Hancock possessed fine business talent, and he was ever alert to promote the interests and to maintain and increase the high reputation of his firm. It was on account of overwork in this capacity that a change of climate became necessary to him. He traveled through New Mexico, California and Montana. While in New Mexico he became interested in the cattle business, and he determined to make his home there, hoping to regain his health and also to build up a profitable business. He settled in Mora county, about fifty miles from Las Vegas, and, with his accustomed energy, entered upon the duties and work before him. In April, 1882, he removed his family to Las Vegas. He had four children, three girls and one boy. The youngest, a girl, died when about nineteen months old.

On New Year's Day, 1883, while engaged in his new and flourishing business, he caught a severe cold. It assumed an acute form, and in a few days it was found necessary for him to go to California, and he started upon the arrival of his father. He was taken to Los Angeles, the

Spanish City of Angels, one of earth's paradises, whither the well, the sick and the aged make pilgrimages. Here he spent the few remaining short days of life, and then passed to the unseen realms above, the eternal paradise.

The many of us who never knew Bro. Hancock, but have followed his exceptionally prosperous career, can with deep emotion join in the heartfelt sympathy of his classmates and friends over his untimely death. No better testimony can be given than that of his friends, and it is with pride and profound respect that we close this notice of our departed brother with the eloquent and just tribute of one of them published in a Dubuque paper soon after his death:

"Here where Mr. Hancock has been known from early boyhood to the present, he was as thoroughly admired among business men, for his rare and ripe excellencies as for his tender heart and purity of life by his family and intimate friends. He was an ambitious man; not selfishly for his own gratification, but that he might increase the sum of human worth in the world. His theory of life was that no one filled the purpose of his birth unless the world was made the better by his existence; and in order to exemplify the full measure of this idea he employed every faculty of his being with all the vigor and intensity of his enthusiastic nature. While his intellect was ever alert with lofty grasping after the highest business prizes, his conscience and moral sensibilities maintained a constant guardianship over his whole life. To say that John S. Hancock bore the esteem of every one who knew him is a truth which no qualifying words can emphasize. Charity never besought him in vain. By his fireside he was peculiarly tender and loving as husband and father, while his devotion to his dear old father and mother was a beautiful illustration of filial affection. His friendships were frank, cordial and enduring. In public life he was the friend of every important enterprise, and many of the thoughts which have been most fruitful for Dubuque's advancement had birth in his active mind. His character was the sun of his life. High minded and noble, we doubt if one ever heard a vulgar or impure word escape his lips. He was an honor alike to his parents, his family, his friends, and to society. He leaves the best of all possessions—the legacy of a pure life and an unsullied character to the young men of Dubuque. May they emulate his example."

The mortal remains of Bro. Hancock were placed in Linwood cemetery, at Dubuque, Iowa, in the same family lot where those of his brother Fennimore, who died in 1872, were placed, and who was also a member of Omega.

VII.

EZRA BENEDICT PARRISH.

DIED MAY 21, 1883.

Aged 35 years, 6 months and 22 days.

Ezra Benedict Parrish was born at Royalton, Berrien county, Mich., on October 29, 1847. His parents were of English descent. His father, Gould Parrish, is a farmer by profession and lives at Stevensville, Mich. Ezra had three sisters and two brothers. Aside from the ordinary schools, he attended the South Bend University, where he prepared for college. In the fall of 1872 he came to Evanston, and entered the Preparatory department with the class of '77. It was at this time that he became identified with Sigma Chi, and was initiated into the Omega chapter, June 2, 1873. Brother Parrish expected to go through the University with his class, but adverse circumstances prevented him, as it did many others at that time, from pursuing his studies farther. He was with the active chapter a short time, and had only a few weeks of the delightful experiences in the fraternity work.

On March 31, 1875, he was married at St. Joseph, Mich., to Miss Ella Whipple. This happy union was blessed with four children, two boys and two girls. The oldest child, a daughter, died in 1879. After his marriage Bro. Parrish, with his young bride, went to Iowa. There they taught in the country schools together for one year. While engaged in this work he was licensed to preach by the M. E. Church. The following year he became principal of the schools at Hastings, Iowa. He remained there two years. Finding a good opening at Malvern, Iowa, he moved his family and served as principal of the schools there as long as his health permitted. His success as a teacher was especially noted, and he was sincerely respected and loved by all his pupils. He was earnest and conscientious in his work, and was always ready as a loyal citizen to do his part in promoting every good cause. During the winter of 1879 he assumed the editorship of the *Malvern Leader*, and soon thereafter he consolidated it with the *Republican*. The last of September, 1881, he gave up his editorial work, took his family to Iowa City and entered the law class of the State University. He worked hard for one year, not heeding the great strain on his mind and body, and completed his course. He graduated June 20, 1882. While at that University he compiled, as class editor, the statistics of his class. There were 139 members of the class, and the document he published is a very creditable one indeed.

Returning to Malvern, he entered into partnership with Hon. W. S. Lewis for the practice of law. He was soon elected mayor of that city, and served in that office until his departure for Dakota. Feeling that his health was failing, he decided to go farther west, hoping to receive some benefit from the change of climate. Having secured a homestead in Douglas county, Dak., he, in company with his brother James, left Malvern in the spring of 1883 with two teams and wagons. They were two weeks on the road. The labor of preparing a house for his family now commenced. There were many trials and discomforts, but through all he seemed hopeful. The climate, however, did not bring the relief expected, and each day he grew more weak. The little house was finished and the family soon joined him. Bro. Parrish had for many years been suffering from dyspepsia. He died very suddenly, and it is believed from congestion of the bowels. On Saturday he had ridden sixteen miles, and on Monday following his spirit had departed. He was laid at rest on his claim in Dakota. He leaves a widow and three small children, the oldest being not quite five years of age. Mrs. Parrish is now living at Stevensville, Mich.

Bro. Parrish united with the Methodist church February 22, 1857, being ten years old. During his life he was a faithful follower of the cross. His work for the Master was always sincere and effective, many times exerting himself beyond his strength. He was a republican, and, when prohibition assumed a prominent part in Iowa politics, he lent his efforts to the cause, and put his whole soul into it. In June, 1882, he delivered a temperance lecture, in which he favored the adoption of the prohibitory amendment to the constitution in strong and forcible terms. He had a good command of language, and was considered a fine orator. As a temperance lecturer he was not excelled in southwest Iowa. In all his life-work Bro. Parrish was a faithful, conscientious man, striving to do right and helping those who were in need. He was kind and loving in his family, and was a devoted husband and father. His work is finished, but the record of it is a glory to his family, his friends, and the Sigma Chi Fraternity.

VIII.

FRANK EDWARD HESLER.

DIED JANUARY 1, 1884.

Aged 32 years, 8 months and 28 days.

Frank Hesler was one of those people of whom it seems impossible to think as dead. Always full of life and spirit, ever the center of whatever activity there was about him, one cannot imagine him silenced and resting forever from life's busy turmoil.

He was born on the third day of April, 1851, at Galena, Ill., being the eldest of eight children. His father, Alexander Hesler, was a photographer, and one of the oldest and best in Chicago. There is a curious little incident connected with his early years that is worth repeating. His father visited the falls of St. Anthony, in May, 1851, when a little hamlet was all that foreshadowed the coming metropolis on its banks, taking with him Frank, then a very little child. One day as they were looking up at the tumbling, rushing waters, Mr. Hesler, moved by an irresistible impulse, lifted the little fellow up under the beautiful spray, giving him a baptism in one of nature's grandest fonts. He little dreamed that beside this spot would spring up the city of Minneapolis, the great wonder of the Northwest, and that it would be the home of his son's future bride.

While on this same visit Mr. Hesler took a daguerreotype view of the Falls of Minnehaha. From this picture Longfellow gained his idea of that beautiful sheet of falling water, which he soon after immortalized in the song of "Hiawatha."

In the course of time the Hesler family came to live in Evanston. Frank commenced his studies in the Preparatory department of the Northwestern University, and afterward entered the University in the classical course. A civil engineering course of study being afterward established, he was the first to register in it. In 1869, while in college, he became a member of Sigma Chi, and into Omega chapter he put his whole soul and enthusiasm. Frank was one of the most active in having the chapter reorganized in 1872. Although engaged in business, he found plenty of time to devote to the fraternity. The chapter did not have a suitable hall, and through his generosity the meetings of the fraternity were held in his father's art gallery. He invented new modes of initiation, putting all his ingenuity into exercise. He fired the whole chapter with his zeal and energy, and to the last day of his life he loved Sigma Chi with an affection that is rare in a man who has been out of college for many years.

When the hand of disease was upon him, and the end not far off, he attended the annual banquet of Omega, at the Union League Club, and, throwing off the sadness that suffering had cast over him, spoke to the boys, with a return of his old fire and enthusiasm, words that they will not soon forget.

When the time of our great Chicago fire came Frank was obliged to leave college with his course of study uncompleted. During 1872 he was with the Chicago, Burlington and Quincy Railroad, doing practical work as a civil engineer. Leaving this position, he wrote for a time in the County Clerk's Office in Chicago. Later, his father established his photograph gallery in Evanston, and Frank became associated with him in business. In the summer of 1873 he visited his old college chum Frank M. Elliot, in Minneapolis. While on this visit he had an opportunity of doing some journalistic work, which was always very congenial to him. He was connected at different times with the *St. Paul Dispatch*, the *Minneapolis Evening Journal*, the *Pioneer Press* and the *New York Tribune*, for which latter paper he reported the Guiteau trial.

Finding Minneapolis a very delightful place, he soon became identified with the young people there. On December 15, 1874, he made his ties to the city still more binding by marrying Miss Ada V. Reid, the only daughter of Hon. A. M. Reid, a prominent and influential citizen. In the winter of 1874 a play, called the "Color Guard," was given at the Academy of Music, for the benefit of the G. A. R. Post, of Minneapolis. Frank Hesler took the leading part in this play, and covered himself with glory. The original intention had been to give only one performance, but its success was so great that it was repeated several nights. He was such a fine actor that he was often urged to go upon the regular stage, where, no doubt, his talent would have made him a fortune.

After his marriage he engaged in the drug business, and afterward in milling. From his early youth he had the desire to be a lawyer, feeling within him the powers for success in that profession. But not until 1881 did he see the way clear to carry out a course of legal study, which he had begun in private at home. He accepted a position in the Fifth Auditor's Department at Washington, and took up the studies in the Columbian Law School, attending lectures morning and evening. His health becoming impaired, he went West in September, 1883, to join the officers of the Canadian Pacific Railway in a trip over their road, sending back racy newspaper reports, as was his custom in all his travels. On his return from this journey his friends saw that the sadness and feebleness which had lately been noticed in him had increased, and soon there was no doubt that he was a victim of the terrible Bright's disease. Everything that could be done to save him was tried — southern air, tender nursing, and the best of medical aid were given, but to no avail. At his Evanston home, as the new year of 1884 came in, he gently passed out of this life with a quiet resignation and trust that were a blessing to those who were left behind. He suffered greatly during his illness. Dr. Noyes very beautifully expressed the idea in his funeral remarks, that, however we might wonder why a young man should be taken off in the very prime of his life, we could not doubt that, as he had gone to a home where he would have no more suffering, but joy forever, the change was right and good for him. After the last services were over, his body was borne to the cars by his Sigma Chi brothers—M. C. Bragdon, E. H. Webster, F. D. Raymond, and F. M. Elliot. He was interred in the family burying lot at Racine, Wis.

Mrs. Hesler received the following letter from Washington soon after his death:

> TREASURY DEPARTMENT, FIFTH
> AUDITOR'S OFFICE,
> WASHINGTON, D. C., January 5, 1884.

MRS. F. E. HESLER—

My Dear Madam—I cannot tell you how sad we have been made this morning by the announcement of your husband's death. It came so suddenly that it has shocked the whole office. I need not tell you that your husband was a great favorite with us—his fund of humor, his genial manners, his close attention to business, and his readiness to help everybody, made him very dear to us all, and our hearts go out to you in this dark hour of bereavement But we are happy in the thought that you are not without support while traversing this valley darkened by the shadow of death. Aside from your faith in God, who never fails to sustain his children in times of trouble and sorrow, the memory of your husband's noble qualities will be of great comfort to you. He was associated with us less than two years, and yet I can say, without hesitation, that we who knew him best *loved him*, while all thoroughly respected him.

As a slight token of our respect, the desk and chair which Frank occupied have been draped, and kind friends added a broken wreath of beautiful flowers, which will be forwarded to you by express.

Around these evidences of our high regard the ladies and gentlemen of the office gathered at an early hour this afternoon, and in a formal manner requested that I extend their sympathy to the wife and family of their dead friend. As a further mark of respect, the office was closed for the remainder of the day.

Sincerely your friend,

D. S. ALEXANDER.

The *Evening Journal* at Minneapolis, in an editorial, spoke of Bro. Hesler in these kind words: "The death of Frank E. Hesler, which occurred on New Year's day, at the home of his father in Evanston, Ill., will carry grief to the hearts of numerous friends in Minneapolis. Mr. Hesler was a young man of brilliant, natural gifts and kindly impulses. He was universally popular. We do not think he had an enemy in the world. At the time he was stricken down with the dread disease that carried him off, his life appeared full of happy promise. The *Journal* extends to the bereaved widow, parents, and other relatives and friends, its heartfelt sympathy in their affliction."

Resolutions appropriate to the occasion were passed and recorded by Omega Chapter, and also by Khurum Lodge, No. 112, A. F. and A. M., at Minneapolis.

To those who knew him, it will be impossible to say enough concerning his good qualities; to those who have never seen him, it is impossible to give an idea of his kindly, manly, Christian character. He loved fun, and kept everyone about him in a happy frame of mind. He was unusually talented, and had unlimited resources within himself. Those who were with him in his college days will always look back with pleasure to the times when he was constantly evolving some new entertainment, for their benefit, from his fertile brain. His home was the scene of some of the most delightful gatherings the young people of those days ever knew. He was a wonderful mimic, and in the little theater which he improvised in his father's attic were given some bits of acting that would have done credit to any performer on a larger stage. Whatever he was doing he entered into with his whole might — be it the planning of an initiation, the surveying of a railroad, or the editing of a paper, and those fortunate ones who were blessed with his friendship found that he was as hearty in that as in everything else.

When quite young he became a member of the Presbyterian Church at Evanston, and throughout life he strove to be consistent with his Christian faith and his early professions.

* * *

CHAPTER XXVI.

LIST OF MEMBERS.

The address and occupation is given on the latest information known to us. The brothers are requested to send to the editor any correction of errors in this list, and report any change of address or occupation at any future time.

LIST OF MEMBERS.

Name.	Class.	Initiated.	Degree.	Occupation.	Address.
Andrews, Edward Wyllys..	1878	Jan. ... 1875	A.B., A.M., M.D	Physician	No. 6 Sixteenth St., Chicago.
Andrews, Frank Taylor...	1881	Jan. 8...1878	A.B., M.D.	do	do
Anderson, Martin Luther..	1877	Oct. 1878	A.B., A.M.	Stock Raising	Ravenswood, Ill.
Appleton, Alanson Stewart	1876	April 21..1873	A.B	Journalist	118 Fifth Avenue, Chicago.
Baker, Holland William *..	1877	Nov. 16..1875	C.E.	Civil Engineer	1415 Washington Ave., St. Louis, Mo.
Beal, Ellery Herbert.......	1872	Charter Member	A.M., A.B., B.D	Minister (M.E. Ch.)	Hinckley, Ill.
Bigelow, James Charles *.	1873		M.D	Minister (M.E. Ch.)	Alden, Ill.
Booth, William Morris.....	1878	Oct. 27...1874	A.M., A.B	Lawyer	152 Dearborn St., Chicago.
Bennett, John W.*.........	1883	Nov. —...1876	B.A.	do	Ann Arbor, Mich.
Bragdon, Merritt Caldwell.	1870	Charter Member.	A.B., A.M., M.D	Physician	Evanston, Ill.
Bragdon, George Erastus..	1872	 1870	Ph. B	Wholesale Grocer	Pueblo, Col.
Burke, James Gurshom...	1872	 1871	A.B.	Lawyer	Aberdeen, D. T.
Bradley, Luther Daniels ..	1874	 1872			Melbourne, Australia.
Brown, W. L...............	1880				Des Moines, Iowa.
Boutell, Evarts (G.........	1874	 1869	LL.B..	Died May 21, 1870.	
Bross, Mason...............	1883	Feb. 23 1879		Lawyer	550 Dearborn Ave., Chicago.
Brown, Harry Putney.....	1883	 1880		Died Dec. 8, 1881.	
Brewer, Frank Miner......	1886	Sept. 15..1881		Physician	Evanston, Ill.
Caddock, Henry	1888	Dec. 19..1884		Student	do
Collins, Lorin Cone.......	1872	Charter Mem.	A.B.	Circuit Judge	County Building, Chicago.
Cooper, Henry Allen......	1873	Feb. 14..1873	Ph. B., LL. B	Lawyer	Racine, Wis.

* Received degree at other institutions.

Name	Year	Date	Degree	Occupation	Address
Condell, John S.	1873			Justice of the Peace	Springfield, Ill.
Currier, Albert Dean	1884	Oct. 5...1880	B.S	Mechanical Engin'r	Boston, Mass.
Crozier, David Edgar	1886	Feb. 2...1883		Student	Princeton, New Jersey.
Clark, Frank Nelson	1858	May 1...1883		Clerk	Omaha, Neb.
Clapp, Charles Lewis	1887	March 21.1884		Farmer	Chillicothe, Ill.
Draper, Charles L	1875	March 10.1874			Jacksonville, Ill.
Davis, Nathan Smith, Jr.	1880	Sept. 24,1875	A.B., A.M., M.D.	Physician.	65 Randolph St., Chicago.
Dale, John Franklin	1880	Jan. ... 1876		Insurance	Omaha, Neb.
Drake, Chester Tuttle	1874	Nov. 11..1873	C.E.	Machinery Manf'r	254 S. Clinton St., Chicago.
Deering, James E.	1880	Oct. ... 1875		Treasurer, Deering Mfg. Co.	Evanston, Ill.
DeGroff, Raymond Victor.	1881		B.S.	Journalist	Sterling, Ill.
Donalson, Dexter Park	1879	Sept. 29..1875	A.B.	Shipping Agt, Deering Mfg. Co.	Evanston, Ill.
Demorest, William Lazier.	1878	Nov. 16. 1875	A.B.	Minister	Redwood Falls, Minn.
Early, Albert Dudley	1877	March 12.1873	A.B.	Lawyer	Rockford, Ill.
Early, Frank Adelbert	1877	May 19 ... 1873		Gen. Agent New England Life Ins. Co.	Detroit, Mich.
Evans, William Gray	1877	June 11..1873	Ph. B.	Real Estate	Denver, Col.
Elmore, Eltinge	1872	June 1874	Ph. B.	Iron Foundry	Milwaukee, Wis.
Elliot, Frank M.	1877	March 12.1873	B.L.	Real Estate	93 Fifth Ave., Chicago.
Etnyre, Charles Dayton	1880	Feb. 14..1877		Abstracts	Oregon, Ill.
Etnyre, Edward Daniel	1881	April .. 1879		Farmer	do
Elliott, Edwin R	1883	Oct. ... 1879		Merchant	Litchfield, Ill.
Eddy, H. C.	1886	Dec. 8.. 1881		Student	Lincoln, Neb.
Frank, Henry	1877	April 22. 1875		Minister	Waseca, Minn.
Foulks, Charles Allison	1880	June 1878	Ph.B.	Physician	Vincennes, Ind.
Gillet, Morrison Monroe	1877	March 17.1873		Com. Traveler	Fond-du-Lac, Wis.
Harris, Frank Mitchell	1875	Feb. 1875	C.E.	Treasurer of Kaw Valley Paint and Oil Co.	1840 Main St., Kansas City, Mo.

LIST OF MEMBERS—Continued.

Name.	Class.	Initiated.	Degree.	Occupation.	Address.
Hamline, John Henry	1875	Jan. 26...1874	A.B., LL.B	Lawyer	Portland Block, Chicago.
Hancock, Fennimore, Enz.	1872			Died Feb. 16, 1872	
Hancock, John S.	1872	June....1869		Died Jan. 19, 1883	
Hesler, Frank Edward	1873	Fall 1869		Died Jan. 1, 1884	
Harrison, Edwin John	1872	June 21..1875	Ph. B	Groceryman	Sauk Center, Minn.
Haskin Walter E.	1873	1871		Manager Golden Eagle Store	Cincinnati, Ohio.
Harris, William Hamilton	1878	Oct. 5..1874	A.B., A.M., LL.B	Lawyer	229 Broadway, New York.
Humphrey, Robert Marshall	1877	Jan. ...1875		Died Aug. 3, 1875	
Hough, Albert S	1874				
Howard, Otis M.	1889	Dec. 19..1884		Student	Evanston, Ill.
Hilton, Theopholus Brown	18-6	Nov. 17..1873	A. B., A. M.	Minister	3537 Bloom St., Chicago.
Hesler, Fred D.	1882	Sept. 28..1878	M. D.	Surgeon U. S. A.	Evanston, Ill.
Hemenway, Francis Wood	1880	Nov. 20..1884		Student	do
Harvey, Robert Hatfeld	1890	Oct. 9...1884		do	do
Ilgenfritz, Charles Alvin	1875	March 10.1873		Nurseryman	Monroe, Mich.
Jessup, Robert Basil	1880	June 11..1877	Ph. B	Physician	Vincennes, Ind.
Knappen, Frank Edward	1877	Oct. 29..1875	A. M., A. B.	Lawyer	Kalamazoo, Mich.
Kampf, Frederick B.	1885	Fall.....1879		Journalist	Wapakoneta, Ohio.
Knox, William M.	1874	Jan. 19..1874	A.B., A.M.	do	123 Fifth Ave., Chicago.
Kline, Lee	1873	1871		Com. Traveler	170 Thirtieth St., Chicago.
Langworthy, Albert Darwin	1870	Charter Mem.	A. B.	Deputy	Sherriff's Office, Chicago.
Lunt, George	1872	Charter Mem.	Ph. B	Grain Commissi'n'r	102 Washington St., Chicago
Lambert, Isaac E.	1875	Feb. 16..1873		Lawyer	Emporia, Kansas.
Lipps, John E.	1880	Dec. 8...1875	Ph. B	Silk Manufacturer	Lyons, France.

LIST OF MEMBERS.

Name			Degree	Occupation	Address
Lathrop, Harry	1885	Sept. 22..1881		Accountant	Greenburg, Ind.
Mathew, Winfield Scott	1876	Sept. 18..1874	A. B., A.M.	Minister	St. Paul, Minn.
Martin, Joseph Earle	1877	Feb. 19..1874		Artist's Materials and Paint	176 Randolph St., Chicago.
Moss, Edmund Stuart	1877	Feb.......1875		Contractor	108 Dearborn St., Chicago.
Merrick, George Peck	1884	Oct. 5.....1880	B. L.	Lawyer	Ulrich Block, Chicago.
McWilliams, Edward	1879	Nov. 16..1875		Merchant	Dwight, Ill.
McWilliams, James Wilson	1879	Oct. 9....1876		do	Odell, Ill.
McFadden, Benj. Lincoln	1889	Oct. 2....1884		Student	Havana, Ill.
Newman, George Peter C.	1873	1870			Hammond, Ind.
Norris, James Shelbourn	1876	1873		Minister	2904 Wells St., Milwaukee.
Owen, Charles	1882	Feb. 11..1879			Boone, Iowa.
Paul, Clarence Richmond	1872	Charter Mem.	A. B.	Private Secretary, Senator Cullom	Washington, D. C.
Pearsons, Henry A.	1862	June 21..1875	A. M.	Farm Loans	Tribune Building, Chicago.
Parrish, Ezra Benedict *	1877	June 2....1873	LL.B	Died May 21, 1883.	
Peck, Harry L.	1887	Nov. 8....1880		Sash and Door Manufacturer	Oskosh, Wis.
Prime, William T.	1886	March 9..1882		Clerk	Dwight, Ill.
Robinson, James Franklin	1872	Charter Mem.	A. B., A. M.	Banker	Rock Island, Ill.
Raymond, Frederic Dwight	1872	1870	A. B.	Gen. Freight Agt. Chicago & Great Southern R. R.	Evanston, Ill.
Randolph, Fred W. *	1881	Spring...1880	LL.B	Died March 11, 1882	
Reihl, Daniel Charles	1874	Feb. 24, 1873	A.B., A.M., B.D.	Minister	Palo, Ionia Co., Mich.
Sparling, William Henry	1872	Charter Mem.	M.D.	Physician	Moawequa, Shelby Co., Ill.
Stewart, Edward Lawrence	1879	Alpha....1876	B.S.	Journalist	120 Fifth Ave., Chicago.
Smith, Henry A.	1880	April 2...1877		Lawyer	1128 S. E. Fourth St., Minneapolis, Minn.
Slichter, Charles Sumner	1885	Nov. 6...1882		Student	Evanston, Ill.
Shuman, Edwin Lewellyn	1887	Oct. 25...1883		do	do

* Received degree at other institutions.

LIST OF MEMBERS—Continued.

Name.	Class.	Initiated.	Degree.	Occupation.	Address.
Springer, Ruter William...	1887	Nov. 9..1882		Student	Evanston, Ill.
Trumbull, Charles.........	1873	1871	C. E.		San Francisco.
Taylor, Fred Manville.....	1876	April 29..1875	A.B., A.M.	Professor	Albion, Mich.
Tunnicliff, George D......	1884	1879		Lawyer	Macomb, Ill.
Watson, Sidney...........	1885	Oct. 12..1882		Student	Evanston, Ill.
Weeden, Bert Miller.......	1889	Nov. 20..1884		do	do
Webster, Edward H........	1875	March 3..1874	M. D.	Physician	do
Wheeler, Charles Pinckney.	1876	Feb. 24..1873	A.B., A.M.	Wholesale Coal.	95 Dearborn St., Chicago.
Wicks, Hamilton Stutely...	1871	Fall 1869	Ph. B	Telephone Co. Organizer.	Coates House, Kansas City, Mo.
Winslow, Frederick C......	1870	June 21..1875	Ph.B., M.D	Physician	Orangeville, Ill.
Wightman, Charles Addison	1885	Oct. 12..1882		Student	Evanston, Ill.
Wallace, Louis Davenport..	1889	Dec. 12..1884		do	do
Yaple, George Lewis.......	1871	Fall 1869	A.M., A.B.	Congressman	Washington, D. C.

Total number of initiates, 116.
Six persons have been expelled.
Total membership of Omega, January 1, 1885, 110.

INDEX.

Alumni Chapters........ 18
Alpha Chapter.. .... 39, 81, 202
Andrews, E. W., 80, 96, 98, 102, 103, 105, 107, 115, 120, 131, 135, 138, 142, 147, 174.
Appleton, A. S., 42, 88, 138, 139, 149.
Anderson, M. L. 94
Adams, I. E......... 100, 101
Andrews, F. T., 102, 111, 112, 115, 120, 123.
Alpha Eta........... ... 129, 131
Alpha Zeta... .. .. 129, 132
Alpha Iota............. 129, 132
A matter of policy...... 161-163

Beal, E. H 31, 136, 138
Bragdon, M. C., 31, 33, 40, 133, 136, 138, 159, 174, 224, 251.
Butler University........... 15
Beloit College, 16; Chapter at......................... 120
Bragdon, G. E., 38, 40, 136, 138, 151.
Beta Theta Pi, 45, 60, 86, 88-92, 96, 98; Reception, 100; Turkey, 112, 117, 156-168, 211.
Booth, W. M., 70, 80, 96, 98, 101, 102, 105, 115, 123, 135, 136, 138, 139, 142, 147, 177.
Brown, W. L................ 87
Bennett, J. W............87, 141
Bear Story, The...... 92, 182-200
Baker, H. W 94
Bross, Mason........ 108, 115, 137
Brewer, F. M 113
Brown, H. P .. 100, 114, 234, 235
Burke, J. G.... ... 136, 138, 140
Blanchard, The Prize........143
Beta Beta Chapter........... 18
Beta Chapter................ 19
Bradley, L. D.............38, 40
Baseball Team, 1871....... ...150
Bristol, F. M........ 166, 173, 176
Bell, T. C.....................211
Boutell, Evarts, G....... 217-225
Boutell, Henry S 218
Baird, Prof. Robert..........224

Constantine Chapter... 19
Collins, Hon. Lorin C., 30, 31, 33, 38, 40, 125, 133, 136, 140, 146, 151, 174, 224, 239.
Columbian University...... 15
College of New Jersey. 15
Cumberland University.. 15, 18
Centre College........ 16
Cooper, H. A, 41, 71, 133, 136, 137, 138, 139, 146.
Colfax, Hon. Schuyler, 88, 89, 92
Crozier, D. E. 104, 118
Convention, Tenth Biennial, 106; Thirteenth Biennial, 111; Report to, 115, 116; Fourteenth Biennial, The, 122-127; Of Sigma Chi, 201-202; Northwestern District, The, 128-132.
Currier, A. D., 110, 112, 120, 121, 137, 139, 142.
Cummings, Rev. Joseph, 24, 117; Remarks of, 125; 180.
Clark, F. N...................118
Chi Chapter............. 129, 131
Chi Chi Chapter 18
Charter Members of Omega, 31
Cumnock, Prof. R. L..... 53, 62
Carbart, Prof. H. S 53, 62
Crist, J. J............... 60, 149
Coleman, L. C............ 60, 149
Caldwell, J. Parks........... 210

Delta Delta Chapter......... 18
Defunct Chapters........ 18
Dixon, Henry St. John...... 18
Delta Kappa Epsilon. 13
Depauw University.... ... 15
Dickinson College 15
Denuison University 15
Drake, C. T............72, 151
Draper, C. L. 83
Davis, N. S., Jr., 84, 107, 135, 137, 138.
Donelson, D. P......84, 107, 137
Deering, Jas. E...87, 141, 159, 177
Dale, J. Frank............... 87
Douthart, S. P............92, 152

261

262 INDEX.

Demorest, W. L..96, 105, 136, 139
De Groff, R. V., 109, 111, 112, 139, 202.
Delta Chapter.................. 18
Delta Upsilon................. 155
Dennis, W. J.................. 214

Evanston 21, 23
Evans, Gov. John........... 22, 94
Erskine College............... 14
Early, A. D., 41, 48, 72, 74, 93, 94, 95, 120, 140, 174, 232.
Etnyre, C. D.................. 88
Elliot, Frank M., 41, 93, 95, 115, 120, 131, 132, 134, 141, 146, 159, 176, 249, 251.
Evans, W. G., 42, 93, 94, 95, 136, 141, 174, 176.
Elliot, E. R...................108
Eddy, H. C....................113
Elliot, Mrs...................118
Elliot Prize..............119, 131
Elmore, Eltinge.....136, 140, 151
Early, F. A................42, 140
Epsilon, Epsilon Chapter.... 18
Epsilon Chapter.............. 18

Fisher, W. L..........19, 129, 207
Fowler, Rev. Charles H., 24, 55, 78, 175.
Frank, Henry..82, 83, 134, 140, 141
Foulkes, C. A........88, 107, 137
Fratres Caros Saluto, a song.104
Fraternity Influence.....156-158
Fosdiek, W. W................. 23

Garrett Biblical Institute, 26, 27
Gillett, M. M......42, 71, 95, 141
Gymnasium, Building a., 87, 94, 174-181
Gamma, Chapter..........14, 20
Gleanings from Old Letters 210-215.

Hillsdale College............. 17
Hanover College.............. 15
Howard College............... 16
Hampden-Sidney College.... 16
Hesler's Gallery..... 34, 39, 40
Hesler, Frank E., 38, 40; Last Speech, 118, 246-254
Hamline, J. H., 48, 83, 115, 133, 138, 139, 146, 149, 159, 167, 174
Harris, W. H., 80, 96, 98, 101, 105, 135, 136, 138, 141, 147, 170
Humphrey, R. M..... 83, 220-234

Harris, Frank M. 83, 133, 141, 167
Hilton, T. B., Jr. 88, 134, 136, 139, 140, 150, 166
Hesler, F. A............106, 107
Hamline, Mrs................. 118
Hamilton, Gov. J. M.... 124, 207
Harrison, E. J., 44, 133, 136, 146, 151
Haskin, W. E................38, 40
Haven, Rev. E. O........ 24, 145
Hancock, Fennimore E., 220, 226-229, 242
Hancock, John S.... 227, 239-242
Hamilton, W. A.............. 230

Illinois Wesleyan University, 17, 113, 118, 172
Indiana State University.... 15
Illinois State University..... 16
Ilgenfritz, C. A 41, 83
Iota Iota Chapter............ 18
Iota Chapter 18
Index, The............. 153, 154
Intercollegiate Literary Association of New York, 164-172

Jefferson College............. 15
Jessup, R. B..... 88, 107, 137, 142
Jordan, Hon. Isaac M., 205, 208, 210

Kappa Kappa, Chapter 18,129,131
Kappa Phi Lambda........... 31
Kenyon College............... 63
Knappen, F. E. 73, 93, 95, 134, 136, 138, 139, 140, 202; as a Warbler, 83-84; His Story, 75-77
Kampf, F. B...................109
Knox, W. M.....133, 138, 141, 146
King Kalakua.................152
Krantz, John, Jr..............177
Kent, Linden.................204

Lunt, Geo. 31, 102, 123, 133, 138, 146, 151, 174, 177, 180.
Langworthy, A. D. 31, 136, 137, 151, 224.
Lagrange College.........14, 214
Lafayette College........... 15
Lambert, I. E..........41, 83, 139
Lipps, John E........87, 107, 180
Lathrop, Harry...............113
Lambda Chapter........202, 203

INDEX.

Massachusetts Institute of Technology.................. 17
Maine University.............. 13
Mississippi College........... 16
Monmouth College........16, 172
McWilliams, E................ 84
McWilliams, Jas. W.........85, 88
Mathew, W. S. 88, 134, 136, 137, 138, 139, 140, 146, 150, 160, 168, 173, 174, 177.
Moss, E. S.................... 94
Martin, J. Earle.............. 95
Marcy, Dr. Oliver.........24, 109
Merrick, Geo. P., 110, 112, 115, 116, 120, 125, 132, 135, 139, 142, 147, 202.
Martin, W. L.................. 60
Muir, Geo. W.................180
Memento Mori—a poem......216

Northwestern University, 21-27; 15, 51, 55, 57, 78; Presidents, 24; Buildings, 25; Condition of, 106, 109; Property, 26; Departments, 28; Future of, 158; Represented in the Inter-Collegiate Literary Association, 165-172.
Northwestern, The...........101
Northwestern Alumni Association....................120
Northwestern, The District Convention............128-132
Norris, Jas. B....83, 137, 138, 141
Nu Chapter................... 18
Necrology 217-254

Omega, located, 21; Poem, 28; Origin, 30; Bowling Alley, 87, 178, 179; Charter Members 31; Chapter House 113, 159, 161; Early Events, 30-37; Total Membership of, 154; Reorganized, 38-46; Banquet of '75, 44; Sleigh-rides, 47-50; Four College Years, 1874-1878, 82-103; History of 1878-1879, 105-107; History of 1879-1884, 108-121; Entertain Fourteenth Biennial Convention, 122-127.
Ohio Wesleyan University.14, 239
Ohio State University........ 16
Owen, Charles.........106, 107

Phi Kappa Psi.......30, 37, 154
Phi Gamma Delta.....30, 53, 55
Paul C. R., 31, 32, 37, 38, 40, 133, 136, 138, 140, 174, 232.
Pennsylvania College........ 15
Polytechnic College......... 15
Purdue University........... 16
Phi Kappa Sigma, 37, 60, 85, 86, 98, 100, 114, 154, 178.
Psi Upsilon Movement ...51-68
Parrish, E. B., 42, 95, 141. 243-246
Peck, H. L....................111
Prince, W. T..................115
Piatt, J. J...............124, 213
Pearson, H. A......44, 140, 159
Phi Chi Chapter.............. 18
Psi Psi Chapter.............. 18
Psi Chapter.................. 18
Prentice, George D........212

Robinson, J. F. 31, 32, 136, 138, 201
Roanoke College............. 16
Randolph-Macon College.... 16
Richmond College............ 16
Reihl, D. C....41, 83, 84, 139, 201
Randolph, F. W., 109, 111-115, 141, 235-238.
Raymond, F. D.......136, 140, 251
Raymond, J. H.........54, 145
Rho Chapter..................202
Runkle, Ben. P..........209, 212
Reynolds, Charles............210

Stevens Institute............ 17
Sigma Chi Fraternity, History of, 13-20; Publications, 19, 67; Government, 20, 67, 102; Character of, 162, 163; Convention, 201; Magazine, 84, 122; Prize Men, 96, 98; Total membership of Omega, 154; History, 111; Bowling Alley, 178, 179; Sentiments, 203-210.
Sparling, W. H............... 31
Southern University......... 16
Smith, H. A.................. 88
Solid Six, The............... 98
Stewart, E. L......106, 107, 202
Slichter, C. S 116, 142, 202
Springer, Ruter W 117
Shuman, Edwin L., 119, 131, 135, 208
Sigma Chapter............... 18
Spade and Serpent Society, 149, 150

Scott, F. H............ 168
Scobey, Frank H.... ... 211, 213

Taylor, F. M., 82, 87, 88, 133, 137, 138, 139, 140, 146, 150, 166, 168, 169, 174, 176, 177, 178
Tripod, The 98, 101, 175
Triumvirs, The......... 102
Tunnicliff, G. D......... .. 109
Theta Chapter........... 129, 132
Theta Theta Chapter. 18
Tucker, Thos. E............. 214

University of Iowa... 17
    "   Nebraska...... 17
    "   Wisconsin..17, 119
    "   Kansas 17
    "   Texas.......... 17
    "   Louisiana..... 17
    "   Mississippi ... 14
    "   Nashville...... 14
    "   Virginia....... 15
University at Lewisburg 15
University of Georgia 15
    "   Michigan....16, 18
    "   Pennsylvania.. 16
    "   Alabama 16
    "   Cincinnati..... 16
Upsilon Chapter 118

Virginia Military Institute.. 17
Vidette, The...................101
Velvet Tops, The............152

Wightman, C. A., 20, 116, 118, 135, 139, 142.
Wakeman, Edgar L.......32, 33
Washington College......... 15
Washington and Lee University 15
Wooster University.......... 16
Wabash College............. 16
Wheeler, C. P., 41, 79, 88, 134, 150, 167, 232.
Webster, E. H............83, 251
Watson, Sidney 116
Winslow, F. C........44, 136, 137
Wicks, H. S..............136, 137
Whipple, J. A. J......60, 150, 177
Warrington, T. C......60, 149
Wooglin and his Dorg.......153
Whale, The 175
Wood, Wallace..............213

XI. Chapter......32, 129, 132, 202

Yaple, George L., 120, 121, 136, 137, 140.

ERRATA.

E. L. Wakeman, of Lambda Chapter, at Bloomington, Indiana.................... 32

Prize 1874. Should be Kaufman in place of Arnold....146
T. M. Warrington............149

www.ingramcontent.com/pod-product-compliance
Lightning Source LLC
Chambersburg PA
CBHW032143230426
43672CB00011B/2435